I0070974

THE LEADER'S PLAYBOOK

CEOs Transforming Vision into Action

Curated by:

THE HERO CLUB

The Leadership Playbook
Curated by C-Suite Network™

Copyright © 2025 by C-Suite Network™. All rights reserved.

No part of this book may be reproduced, stored in a retrieval system, or transmitted in any form or by any means—electronic, mechanical, photocopying, recording, or otherwise—without the prior written permission of the publisher, except in the case of brief quotations embodied in critical reviews and certain other noncommercial uses permitted by copyright law.

Cover Design and Interior Design by Michael Beas
Published by Atlas Elite Publishing
Powered by the C-Suite Network

www.atlaselitepublishingpartners.com

www.c-suitenetwork.com

Paperback ISBN: 978-1-962825-53-5

This book is a work of nonfiction. Every effort has been made to ensure the accuracy of the information presented. However, the publisher and authors disclaim any liability for errors or omissions.

Images, data, and references cited in this book have been used with permission or fall under fair use guidelines.

For permissions or inquiries, contact C-Suite Network™.

Table of Contents

The Beginning

The Hero Club is a values-based organization for CEOS, founders and investors that pledge to lead with integrity, transparency, share their success and give back to their communities. This invitation-only group puts humanity at the forefront of all they do, and the metrics of success are measured beyond profits alone.

Along with operational excellence, this enables business executives to grow faster, smarter, and more sustainably. Together, we empower great leaders with the right resources, relationships, education, and experiences to drive change and take our member companies to the next level.

The C-SUITE NETWORK™ acquired The Hero Club in 2016 from Rob Ryan. He earned national attention when he grew his 1989 start-up company, Ascend Communications, to more than $2 billion in sales by the late 90's. Lucent Technologies acquired Ascend in 1999 for approximately $20 billion in what was termed at the time the "largest technology merger ever." In fact, until Microsoft bought LinkedIn for $26.2 billion in

December of 2016, it remained the biggest sale of a single tech company for 17 years!

Rob had a belief that he should give back and he did. When he sold his company, he set aside 10% of the ownership to be given to employees -- $2 billion in one day. Thus, setting a record for the making the most of millionaires in one single day.

Here's the part of the story that many don't know about.

Mr. Ryan is a creature of habit. One day, having lunch at a local café (the same café where a soon-to-be blockbuster movie was being filmed – "Mrs. Doubtfire," starring Robin Williams). So, when he stepped outside the café after lunch, he was not surprised to see a line of people waiting for what he assumed were fans wanting a photograph or the autograph of the megastar comedian and actor.

But they weren't.

They were there to see him.

It was a gathering of his employees who knew his lunch plans and spotted his car with its signature license plates "Ascend 1" (his wife having "Ascend 2") in the café parking lot. It was their chance to speak to the CEO of the company.

When he stepped out to the afternoon sun, they started to clap and shake his hand, patting him on the back. He confronted them asking why he was the "object of all this special attention," this happiness and joyful adulation?

To recognize him as being a hero.

One by one they stepped up. To tell them their very personal stories of how his sharing would change their lives.

The day he sold the company, unlike some other CEOs, he didn't take the money and run. He shared it with the people who helped him make the company successful. That day in 1999, he made janitors, night watchmen, secretaries, and so many others millionaires overnight. He didn't have to do any of this. He was under no obligation to share the wealth; yet he did. Two billion dollars is a lot of money. More than two decades ago, that was an even bigger amount of money.

This act would enable Mr. Ryan's many employees to pay for their kids' (or grandkids') education, an operation for a loved one and even pay off people's mortgages. Over and over, they kept telling him, "Mr. Ryan, you are our hero!"

This is the foundation of The Hero Club — that leadership is not just about scaling and profits, but about lifting others as you rise and doing business in a way that honors people, purpose, and performance. That day outside the café reflected what we all strive for: to be remembered not just for what we built, but for how we led.

The Hero Club exists to carry forward that same spirit: to redefine what it means to be a successful business leader. We're not just building companies. We're building legacies. When you lead with integrity, elevate others, and measure success by the lives you impact, you don't just create wealth —

you create meaning. That's the standard we hold. That's the Hero's path.

Find out more by visiting our website:
https://pages.c-suitenetwork.com/hero-club

Foreword

By Jeffrey Hayzlett

There's a saying I've always liked: *Begin with the end in mind.* That's not just a great piece of advice, it's a damn good strategy for how to lead, how to live, and how to build something that actually matters.

If you're holding this book, *The Leaders Playbook: CEOs Transforming Vision into Action,* then chances are you're not just interested in leadership, you're living it. Or trying to. And let me tell you, I've been there. In the boardrooms, in the trenches, in the good days and the gut-wrenching ones. Leadership is more than a title, it's a mindset. It's how you show up.

Start With the Why -- and Then the How

When I think about my own approach to strategic planning and leadership development, it always starts with a simple question: *Where the hell are we going?* If you don't know the destination, how can you lead anyone there?

Start with that vision. What does success look like? Feel like? Who's with you? Why are you even going in that direction?

What's the mood, the attitude, the vibe? Because make no mistake, your values drive your culture, and your culture drives your outcomes.

Your mission statement must be something bigger (and more permanent) than a pretty PowerPoint slide you show at a company meeting. It's about defining what I call your COS -- your Conditions of Satisfaction. What kind of leader do you want to be? How do you want people to feel when they work with you, buy from you, follow you?

Then you evaluate. Do you have the skillset to make it happen? That's where a lot of leaders screw up. They assume ambition alone will get them to the corner office. It won't. You have got to look at your capabilities the same way you would run a go-to-market plan or a SWOT analysis. What are your strengths? What are your blind spots? Where do you need backup?

Same process. Same evaluation. Same approach. And when done right? Very predictable outcomes.

Be the Most Strategic Person in the Room

Now, let me tell you something I've learned from one of the smartest marketers I know....who also happens to be my son Tyler. And I'm not saying that just because he is my kid. He's sharp. And you know why? Because he asks the most important question in business: *What problem are we solving?*

That helps cut through all the noise.

It's easy to get into the mode of just *doing*. Meetings, emails, plans, more meetings. But if you don't stop and ask, "Why the hell are we doing this?" -- then you're just spinning wheels. Leaders forget this all the time. They confuse activity with progress.

Your job as a leader isn't to be the smartest person in the room, it's to be the most strategic. Your role is to channel every resource, from people, money, budgets, inventory, and time, into momentum. And time? That's your most valuable asset. Not your P&L. Not your brand equity. Not even your Rolodex. Time is the one thing you can't make more of.

Use it wisely. Protect it fiercely.

One aspect of business many people fear, and not unreasonably so, is failing at something. Let's talk about failure for a second. Because if you are going to transform vision into action, you are going to fail. A lot. And often. Especially if you're pushing boundaries and innovating.

One of the best pieces of advice I ever read came from a book that asked the question: *Is anyone going to die?* I carry that with me to this day. When things go south, and they will, I remind myself: we are not on the battlefield. No one's dying. We will figure it out.

Lynn Martin, the CEO of the Intercontinental Exchange, said AI will be the biggest disruptor we have ever seen. She talked about a business model where they had an $80 billion market cap but only 20 percent of the employees they once needed.

That is not just innovation, that is a complete recalibration of what business looks like. That is the kind of shift that breaks old models and builds new empires.

So yeah, you will fail. Failing sucks. But there's nothing wrong with it; in fact, it could be our greatest teacher. What you want is to *fail fast*. Learn fast. Adjust. Move. And always ask: what's the worst-case scenario? Is anyone going to die? If the answer's no, then saddle up and keep going.

People love asking me, "Jeffrey, what's your biggest failure?" You know what I say? *I don't know yet.* I've had plenty. Big ones. Public ones. But if I'm doing my job right, if I'm really scaling, then my biggest failure is probably still ahead of me. Because growth does not come from safety. It comes from risk. From bold moves. From putting your neck on the line.

Every day, you are going to face decisions that could go sideways. Every. Single. Day. That's the price of admission when you're in the game at the highest level.

You get hit. You get knocked back. Mike Tyson said it best: *Everyone has a plan until they get punched in the face.* And business? It punches hard and sometimes, repeatedly.

But you know what? This too shall pass. That's another phrase I live by. The highs don't last. Neither do the lows. Just ride the wave, keep paddling, and keep your eyes on the horizon.

I've been on numerous stages for keynotes and many boardrooms across multiple industries. I am asked what inspired me to become an entrepreneur. Truth is, I can't imagine doing anything else. It's in my blood. It's who I am. It's the last thing I think about when I go to bed at night, and the first thing I think about the moment I wake up.

Now, I believe leaders and entrepreneurs are born, but they can also be taught. The life of an entrepreneur is shaped by many aspects of life such as their upbringing, their environment, their choices. But I also believe there's a fire inside the great ones that you just can't teach. It's a spark. A restlessness. A hunger to build something that wasn't there before. It's almost like a (not so) secret society of people you meet along the way where you know that's exactly what they're doing. They're fueled by that passion, persistence and perseverance.

We embrace the free enterprise system not because it's easy, but because it's ours. American enterprise has been a model to emulate throughout history and continues to find ways to innovate and adapt to the changing landscape of business. What makes it so great? That feeling of freedom and drive and responsibility that races through our veins. We didn't plan this life. We didn't study for it. We *became* it.

And yeah, as we get older, we add more zeroes, and we move faster -- but the game is the same. Risk, reward, repeat.

Some people just know. You look across a room, you see someone, and you just *know*. They've got it. No decoder ring needed. It's like a secret language for those of us who lead and create and refuse to settle.

So, what's the real playbook for leaders?

- **Begin with the end in mind.** Every single time.
- **Ask better questions.** What problem are you solving? Why are you doing this?
- **Be strategic.** Use your resources wisely. Protect your time.
- **Expect failure.** Learn fast. Adjust faster.
- **Embrace the journey.** There's no final destination—only the next move.

This book is filled with CEOs who understand that. Who live it. They've taken vision and turned it into action. Not through luck. Not through perfect plans. But through grit, clarity, and courage.

That's what it takes. That's what this playbook is about.

And if you're ready to play at that level, if you're ready to lead in a way that actually changes the game then turn the page.

Your journey starts now. Let's go.

Jeffrey Hayzlett

A Maverick in Global Business and Leadership

Jeffrey Hayzlett is a global business celebrity, esteemed speaker, and former Fortune 100 C-Suite executive, recognized for his bold strategies, marketing brilliance, and entrepreneurial spirit. With a career that spans decades, Hayzlett has left an indelible mark on businesses of all sizes—from startups to global enterprises—by driving transformational change and leveraging innovative leadership.

As a pioneer in using corporate platforms to elevate brand visibility and drive revenue, Hayzlett earned the title of "The Celebrity CMO" by *Forbes* for his groundbreaking work in marketing and media. During his tenure as a Fortune 100 officer, he demonstrated the power of executive leadership in influencing enterprise growth through innovative branding and communication strategies.

Hayzlett is also a prolific speaker, captivating audiences from the age of eight, when he first took the stage as the emcee of his second-grade play. Since entering professional speaking in his 20s, he has delivered hundreds of keynote speeches annually, sharing his expertise with leaders worldwide. In 2015, he was inducted into the National Speakers Association's prestigious Hall of Fame, joining an elite group that includes General Colin Powell, Zig Ziglar, and Ken Blanchard.

Currently, Hayzlett hosts the widely acclaimed podcast and TV show, *All Business with Jeffrey Hayzlett,* on C-Suite Radio and C-Suite TV. He has also appeared on nearly every major global news network, including NBC, CBS, ABC, FOX, CNBC, MSNBC, Canada's CBC, and the UK's BBC, as well as networks in Israel, China, Japan, and beyond.

As a four-time best-selling author, Hayzlett has penned transformative business books such as *The Mirror Test, Running the Gauntlet, Think Big Act Bigger,* and *The Hero Factor,* offering actionable insights for leaders striving to make a meaningful impact. His thought leadership extends beyond the page, with his dynamic speaking engagements energizing audiences to embrace change, drive growth, and foster innovation.

With accolades that include induction into five business halls of fame, Hayzlett stands as one of the most sought-after business minds in the world. Whether advising executives, appearing as a media commentator, or mentoring the next generation of leaders, he embodies a relentless commitment to helping others succeed.

Drawing inspiration from his cowboy roots, Hayzlett brings grit, determination, and a no-nonsense approach to everything he does—making him a true maverick in the ever-evolving world of business.

LinkedIn: https://www.linkedin.com/in/hayzlett/
Facebook: https://www.facebook.com/JeffreyHayzlett
X: https://x.com/JeffreyHayzlett
Insta: @jeffreyhayzlett

Chapter One

Vision, Vulnerability, and the Courage to Lead

Amy Bohn

Heroic leadership isn't about commanding attention. It's about choosing the brave path—especially when it's uncomfortable. It's about daring to lead with vision, vulnerability, and hope. As a CEO, I've discovered that effective leadership demands much more than intellect and execution. It demands soul. It demands the willingness to grow through adversity and to be shaped by the people and purpose you serve.

Some of my greatest breakthroughs have come from moments of stillness—on airplanes, between the clouds—when clarity finds me and strategy flows. That time disconnected from constant notifications gives way to creative freedom. I've been known to land with an entire roadmap for the quarter scribbled across a napkin. The important thing isn't the altitude. It's the space to envision something better and the belief that your team can bring it to life.

Leadership, at its best, begins with vision—but it's sustained by intention. My approach to planning is deeply rooted in visualization. I don't just think about where we're headed—I feel it, speak it, and build it into every step we take. The clearer my belief in what's possible, the more others around me believe it too. Strategy is more than milestones and objectives; it's the story we tell ourselves about where we're going and why it matters.

But belief alone isn't enough. We need structure to reach that vision. That's where we build the map, define each person's role, and ensure clarity in execution. Accountability thrives where direction is clear. I've learned to combine radical honesty with radical encouragement. Feedback should lift, not crush. Even in correction, there is space for belief in a person's ability to rise.

A vital part of my philosophy is this: leadership is about transformation. And transformation requires disruption. That disruption might come in the form of a bold new idea or the courage to walk away from a safe, familiar pattern. It sometimes comes by defying the status quo and inspiring people towards change. I believe the world needs fewer leaders playing it safe and more principled leaders willing to speak the uncomfortable truth and act with courage.

My great aunt showed great acts of courage. During World War 2, she lived in Budapest, Hungry. In the face of tyranny and risking death, she dressed up as a beggar to gather extra food for Jewish families hiding in a cave close by. I follow her example of bold, courageous, fearless, and transformative leadership.

True leadership isn't about avoiding failure. It's about learning how to rise. I've failed. I've experienced loss and disappointment that took me to my knees. When my parents' home of almost 30 years burned down in early 2024, everything we held dear—photos, memories, heirlooms—was gone in minutes. I grieved hard the loss of my childhood home and the irreplaceable. But I also chose to stand again. And I let that experience shape me. I shared my story with my friends, colleagues, and audiences across the country—not to garner sympathy, but to show that leadership includes suffering. It includes the courage to be human.

We grow not in spite of pain, but because of it. I'm not a stranger to pain. I experienced a devasting life altering injury almost 9 years ago. After suffering a spinal injury, the doctors said I had a 50% chance of dying and an 80% chance of being paralyzed. During this time, I lost the ability to walk or talk. Nothing in my body worked like it used to. My nervous system was injured. A simple task like lifting a water bottle or cutting an apple became arduous. After a long road of recovery, 2 years later, I had a brain injury as well. The brain injury created many additional challenges and high levels of pain.

Each time I stand on a stage to deliver a speech or interview on a podcast, it's a miracle. Both that I can walk and that I can talk. My traumatic brain injury created cognitive decline and impairments. My ability to read out loud was reduced to a few minutes at a time. Words floated away from my brain's memory and the formulation of thoughts or ideas was impaired. Dysphagia enveloped me as my once effortless ability to speak was now delayed. I've learned patience as healing happened over the course of years.

As I've continued to live with daily pain and residual issues from both injuries, I learned we can channel pain into our legacy. I believe when we embrace our legacy, we can transform the impossible into the possible. That belief, tenacity, and resilience helped me heal and become a better leader. External successes and public victories are preceded by the personal victories. I hold on to the ability to be resilient. Resilience is the bridge between our lowest valleys and our greatest triumphs.

Failure teaches us the language of courage. Every challenge also has infinite possibilities to solve it. It invites us to assess what we truly value and to lead with clarity and humility. Failures provide an opportunity for renewal, rebirth, and expansion. I hope to inspire and influence others in their life journey to know there's light despite the darkest times and hope in spite of the unknown. I've come to see setbacks as sacred crossroads—places where we're invited to either stay stuck or step forward. I choose forward.

Another cornerstone of my leadership is emotional intelligence. With a background in psychology, I've long understood the power of perception. Our ability to lead hinges on our ability to listen—to body language, to tone, to unspoken signals. EQ is a superpower. It allows us to sense disconnection before it escalates. It gives us the grace to respond rather than react.

Emotional intelligence isn't just about reading others. It's about being aware of ourselves. When we learn to manage our own emotions, we stop making decisions out of fear or frustration. We gain the clarity to lead with empathy and the discipline to wait when the moment calls for patience. In practice, EQ is the filter I use to assess every difficult conversation, every hiring decision, every partnership. It allows me to choose wisely, not react impulsively.

As a leader, I carry the belief that success never happens in isolation. Leadership is relational. You cannot build a successful company without investing in the relationships that make it thrive. Clients, team members, partners—they are people with stories, goals, fears, and dreams. When we learn to connect with them on that level, everything changes.

And perhaps most importantly, leadership is also deeply personal. I'm a mother, a wife, and a woman of faith. I believe in protecting the things that matter most. That's why I remind those I lead: "We cannot save the world if we lose our families along the way." My family comes first. Always. And I want the same for my team. Our work is a reflection of our lives—not the other way around.

So, I prioritize personal balance, not perfection. I build in resets. I pause when the balance tilts too far. Whether through walking, journaling, prayer, or simply having an honest check-in with my family—I return to center. Strength comes not from doing it all, but from knowing when to pause, when to breathe, and when to begin again. It's all about maintaining personal balance synergized with finding the ways to keep that balance together.

Hero leadership is about more than metrics. It's about how you show up. It's about creating space for others to become more of who they are. It's about bringing light into dark places, even when you feel like you're still finding your own way. It's about choosing growth when fear whispers that staying the same would be easier.

We live in a world that needs brave leaders—people who lead with heart, with conviction, with vision. My hope is that every time I step into a room, speak on a stage, or connect with my team, they feel that light. That invitation. That belief that inspires change.

To be a hero leader is not to be perfect. It's to be persistent. It's to keep showing up, again and again, even when the path is unclear. It's to believe that your leadership matters. And that by leading with intention and courage, you can change everything.

Because leadership isn't just what you do. It's who you become in the process.

Scan the QR code to listen to my interview on
"C-Suite Success with Tricia Benn."

About the Author

Amy Bohn

Amy Bohn is the co-founder and President of PERK, a non-profit. Amy is originally from Arkansas and has a degree in psychology and a background in life coaching, working with people of all walks of life. Her leadership has impacted people of all ages. As an activist leader in California, Amy speaks across the state and the country on issues encouraging and teaching people how to protect their children, preserve parental rights, and defend our freedoms.

Amy brings hope as a professional speaker at rallies, events, news interviews, inspiring and empowering people to fight for their freedoms, helping them remember their own power to take effective and decisive action. Amy is the mother of three beautiful children and married to the love of her life for 24 years. Amy loves Thai food, writing music, and sunsets.

As the President of PERK, Amy leads a non-partisan, non-profit whose mission is to advocate for medical freedom, bodily autonomy, children's rights, parental rights, civil rights, and protecting children's right to an education. Amy had led PERK to achieve its mission through educational outreach, action, advocacy, litigation, and policy awareness. PERK has tens of thousands of members throughout California, consisting of parents of children attending school, public employees, first responders, and concerned citizens. Amy has led PERK to develop advocacy programs for veterans, first responders, parents, children, teachers, with a positive impact on millions of people. She is a leader among leaders building coalitions and task forces that accomplish what's needed. She is fearless addressing the mandates and challenging the issues that undermine fundamental constitutional rights. Amy led PERK to file numerous lawsuits in California. The pressure of their litigation has led to the protection of citizens, first responders and public employees' jobs preserved, parental rights, and medical freedom. For more than 5 years, Amy continues to lead PERK to be instrumental in influencing and leading historic victories in California.

SOCIAL:
X: @Amy_L_Bohn
LinkedIn: https://www.linkedin.com/in/amy-bohn-60914b210/
Website www.perk-group.com

Chapter Two

Leading as a Hero Leader

Robert Pizzini

The essence of leadership is not found in power, status, or authority—it is found in the unwavering commitment to elevating those around you. A hero leader does not merely direct; they inspire, cultivate, and empower their team, ensuring that every individual is aligned with the vision of the organization while also growing on their own unique path.

Core Values: The North Star of Leadership

Great leadership begins with core values. They are not just words on a poster or a section in the employee handbook—they are the guiding principles that dictate every action, every decision, and every interaction within an organization. As a retired Navy Special Operations Officer and a business leader, I have seen time and again that without clear and meaningful core values, an organization drifts aimlessly. When everyone on the team is keenly aware of the vision, they can determine how each employee, team, department, etc., can best contribute to the vision. This will lead to more specific goal setting at the tactical, customer facing level as well as management levels such as Sales and Marketing, Maintenance, and Professional Development to name a few.

For me, loyalty, integrity, and professionalism serve as the North Star. I do not define these for my team—rather, I expect them to embody these principles in their own way. Core values must be simple and actionable. You have to start with core values that are meaningful. Companies that bog themselves down with six or more values, each with paragraphs of definitions, miss the mark. If an employee cannot recite and apply the organization's core values at a moment's notice, those values are not ingrained in the culture.

A hero leader builds a culture where these values are not just stated but lived daily. They become the foundation of trust, ensuring that every team member feels valued and supported in both their professional and personal development. Core values also help an organization stay resilient in the face of adversity. When challenges arise, a strong foundation of values enables a team to remain unified and focused on their mission.

Vision and Goal Setting: Creating the Roadmap to Success

A leader without a vision is like a ship without a rudder. At my organization, I use a structured approach to ensure that every individual, team, and department contributes meaningfully to our overall mission. We utilize the military quad chart—a four-quadrant system that outlines our Mission and Vision (our core values), Culture, Focus Areas, and Goals. Goal setting begins with a vision. This ensures that goal setting is not just an exercise in management, but an actionable process tied directly to our long-term success. Goals must be tangible and measurable.

Each Fall, my leadership team convenes to update our annual strategy. As the owner and leader, I have to ensure our goals are realistic, relevant, and rigorous. Input comes from all levels of the organization, ensuring that the team is considering all relative information. A true leader listens, learns, and adjusts, fostering a culture where employees feel invested in the company's direction. Leadership is not about making every decision alone; it is about empowering others to take ownership of their role in achieving the shared vision. A team that actively participates in defining its objectives is more engaged, accountable, and driven to succeed. I have learned that some of the best ideas for improvement come from my customer facing, front line teammates. Not every idea is executable, so I ask three questions when faced with good ideas or recommendations to improve: 1. Will it enhance the employ experience? 2. Will it enhance the customer experience? 3. Will it enhance the bottom line? If the answer is yes to all three, we are doing it. If the answer is yes to 1 or 2 of the three, we will take a closer look at the possibilities.

Trust and Empowerment: The Secret to Innovation

Many organizations claim to value innovation, but few create an environment where it can thrive. Fear of failure is the greatest enemy of progress. Too many employees hesitate to take risks because they believe mistakes will be met with reprimands rather than learning opportunities.

In my leadership approach, I emphasize calculated risk-taking. I expect my team to assess risks, make informed decisions, and execute boldly. When things don't go according to plan, this is where you must stand with your folks and get them in motion again and encourage them to move forward stronger. In the military, leaders are trained, tested, and trusted to act. Business leaders should take the same approach.

If an employee feels that leadership does not have their back, they will avoid risks altogether, which stifles innovation and long-term growth. Your teammates must know that you have their backs. If there is a lack of complete trust, people may not think and act bold on the company's behalf, for fear of being reprimanded or even fired. A hero leader cultivates a culture where bold action is encouraged and supported. An organization that values trust and open communication fosters an environment where employees feel safe to present new ideas and challenge the status quo. Without trust, innovation withers.

Balancing Work and Well-Being: The Leader's Responsibility

A leader's ability to perform is directly linked to their health and wellness. I adhere to what I call the General Leadership Law, which states that rest, hydration, nutrition, exercise, brain-heart link, and lifelong learning are so interconnected that a change in one, positive or negative, will have a corresponding change on all others. For example, if I am not well rested, hydrated, and nourished, the exercise I perform will not benefit my brain and heart as much as it would have had I first addressed these three factors. After all, the health and communication between the brain and heart control every thought, spoken word, and every movement, on the job and while not at work.

Throughout my 26 years in US Navy Special Operations I have seen, and personally experienced, time and time again, the high performance of individuals and teams that focus on these aspects of health and wellness. The key is to enable. Leaders must model this behavior. I provide gym memberships, have a modestly equipped workout area within my business, provide access to a private gym right next to my facility, and frequently ask about workout activity and other learning initiatives. At my quarterly All Hands, I invite everyone to share what they are doing to maintain and advance health and wellness and encourage group fitness activities. We also ensure to have direct discussions with each other and realize that the "human condition" is ever present. We all have an off day. We all have a car that must to go to the shop, children with varying needs, a sick parent perhaps, death in the family, and other aspects of life that interfere with work. By embracing your teammates and helping them through these potentially tough times, we are being great leaders and teammates and the trust factor couldn't be any better.

A well-rested, well-nourished, and mentally sharp team will always outperform one that is burned out and disengaged. Leaders who neglect their own well-being set a dangerous precedent—one that leads to high turnover, low morale, and ultimately, poor performance.

Mental resilience is just as important as physical health. A leader who maintains clarity of mind, emotional intelligence, and a sense of balance will be far more effective than one who is constantly operating in survival mode. Self-care is not a luxury—it is a necessity for sustained excellence.

Knowing When to Forgive and When to Fire

One of the toughest decisions a leader faces is determining when to support an employee's growth versus when to part ways. My philosophy is simple: if an individual is aligned with our core values and acts in good faith, they deserve the opportunity to learn from their mistakes. A lesson I have learned is to know when to forgive and when to fire. Beyond the paycheck, people want to like what they do, feel that their efforts are significant in achieving company objectives, be recognized as expert in what they do, and are proud to work for your organization. However, when behavior consistently undermines the organization's culture, no amount of performance can compensate.

High performance with low behavior is a poison to any organization. I have made the mistake of holding on to toxic high-performers for too long, and when they were finally let go, the overwhelming response from the team was relief. A hero leader must make tough calls, not just for the bottom line, but for the integrity of the team.

Conversely, when an employee demonstrates strong behavior and values but struggles with performance, a leader should assess whether additional training, mentorship, or a role adjustment could help them thrive. Great leadership requires discernment—the ability to recognize when someone needs guidance and when it is time to let go. We all make mistakes in the workplace. But if the employee has bought into the mission of the organization and has acted in with good intent, then provide them with a path to recover from the mistake. I call this forgiven vs. fired.

The Path Forward: Leading with Purpose

Hero leadership is not about commanding—it is about serving. It is about creating an environment where employees feel safe to take risks, empowered to grow, and motivated to contribute their best. Great culture produces great teammates who perpetuate great culture. It is about leading with integrity, making decisions with purpose, and never losing sight of the human element of business.

For those stepping into leadership roles, my advice is simple: Stay focused. No matter the obstacles, keep your eyes on your long-term vision. And most importantly, take care of yourself so that you can continue to take care of others. Pay attention to your health and wellness.

A true hero leader does not seek recognition—they seek impact. And in doing so, they build organizations that thrive long after they are gone. Leadership is a continuous journey—one that requires dedication, self-reflection, and an unwavering commitment to the success of others. As you move forward in your leadership journey, remember that your greatest legacy will not be what you built, but who you inspired.

Scan the QR code to listen to my interview on "C-Suite Success with Tricia Benn."

About the Author

Robert Pizzini

Robert Pizzini is the Managing Partner and Chief Executive Officer of iFLY Va Beach Indoor Skydiving. He brought this multimillion-dollar technology to Virginia Beach in 2015. In 2018 iFLY Va Beach was awarded the Chamber of Commerce Small Business of the Year. In 2019, Robert launched Elevate Your Leadership, a leadership experience that refreshes and energizes seasoned executives, develops new leaders, and builds high performing teams. In 2022, he authored his first Best Selling book titled Elevate Your Leadership, how to develop, Maintain, and Advance Lifelong Leadership. Robert's efforts earned the Hampton Roads Chamber of Commerce Leadership Award.

Robert retired from the U.S. Navy in 2010 after 26 years of service in Navy Special Operations as a Master Explosive Ordnance Disposal (EOD) Technician, and EOD Officer. He completed a combat tour with the Combined Joint Special Operations Task Force, Arabian Peninsula, Balad, Iraq. His personal decorations include the Bronze Star.

Mr. Pizzini received his Bachelor of Science in Liberal Arts from New York Regents College and graduated from Troy State University with a Master of Science degree in International Relations and National Security. He is also a graduate of Air Command and Staff College and was an adjunct professor with American Military University's School of Homeland Security from 2007-2010.

Professional affiliations include Executive Committee, Hampton Roads Chamber of Commerce, and board member of The Warrior for Life Fund. Robert is a USA Hockey Level 4 coach, and coaches high school hockey.

LinkedIn: http://www.linkedin.com/in/elevateyourleadership

Chapter Three

Transforming Your Organization Through Credibility

C. Lee Smith

One of my first bosses told me that having a reputation for being smart, honest and hardworking would define my professional success just as much as last month's results. He said that whatever I said would have little impact if the other person doesn't see me as credible first. It made sense then, but it became even more clear once I took on my first leadership role.

As the leader, you are a convenient target for anyone who has been fired for not doing their job, gets a win from seeing you lose (both inside or outside your company) or thinks your company is horrible because it doesn't align with their political beliefs.

The naysayers' need for clicks, views and likes from an audience with a sympathetic ear supersedes the need to be objective, accurate or well-informed. Their noise can be a drag on your credibility if enough people listen to them. But they will have little effect if you publicly demonstrate your competency, authenticity and congruency.

Before we go any further, let's define credibility. In general terms, a credible person is someone you can consistently rely on for guidance and information you can use to make better decisions in your everyday life. In the context of leadership, credibility is what enables your words, ideas and actions to be taken seriously.

Some leaders mistakenly think building credibility is the same thing as building trust. Credibility is a pathway to trust. In fact, it's a prerequisite. You can have credibility without having someone's trust. But you cannot have trust without credibility.

Simply put, if you want to win the trust of investors, board members and partners, start by establishing your credibility with them. If you want to inspire and motivate your employees, start by being mindful of how what you say impacts their ability to take what you say at face value.

But there's a problem…

The credibility of corporate CEOs is alarmingly low.

Other than salespeople and members of Congress, no other group in the U.S. suffers from lower credibility than CEOs of large organizations, according to the results from the 2023 State of Credibility in America study by SalesFuel.

The research found that only 26% of U.S. adults believe CEOs of large companies are credible. It's easy to be discouraged by these findings, but I see them as an opportunity for you to stand out as a leader.

Perhaps there is something to be learned by looking downstream. Small-to-midsize business owners have done a much better job of establishing credibility in the marketplace with 63% of all U.S. adults giving them high scores. 69% of men agree these owners are credible. However, only 58% of women agree, while the number is slightly higher for Black Americans at 61%. These numbers are quite high when compared to the general sentiment about corporate CEOs.

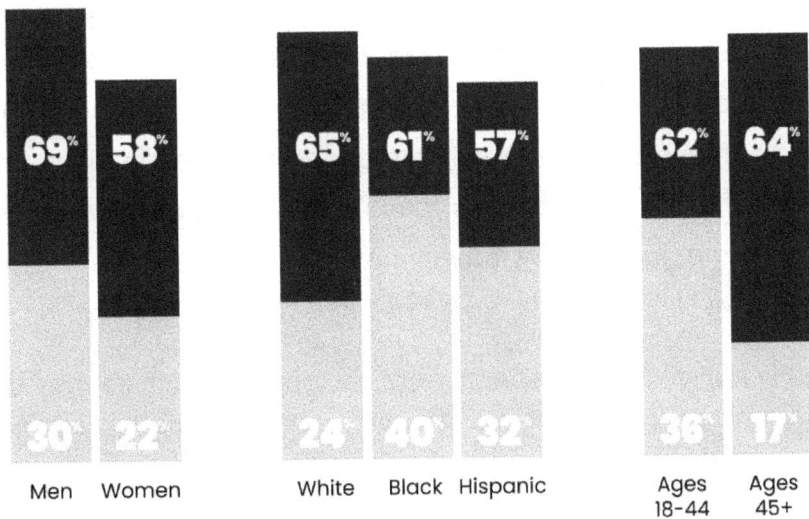

69%	58%		65%	61%	57%		62%	64%
30%	22%		24%	40%	32%		36%	17%
Men	Women		White	Black	Hispanic		Ages 18-44	Ages 45+

■ "Small and midsize business owners are credible."
  "CEOs of publicly traded companies are credible."

Why the huge difference in credibility between SMB owners and CEOs of large organizations?

I believe it comes down to being known, being accessible and having a bias toward service.

Consumers often personally know the owners of SMBs, who show an obvious expertise and passion for what they do. Consumers generally see these company leaders as knowing what they're talking about, knowing how to help and as businesspeople who will do what they promise – not someone who will do or say anything to boost earnings.

Your credibility impacts your company's sales.

The CEO has to be the best salesperson in the company. As the leader, people check you out online long before they reach out to you in person. I'm not just talking about the media but also your investors, partners, employees, and their families. The same holds true for your company's customers, and what they find online impacts whether they will take the next step, according to SalesFuel's Voice of the B2B Buyer survey.

Nearly half of B2B prospects want to know as much as they can about the business they might buy from. Understanding whether you have experience helping clients in their industry is a key concern, and to find out, they'll review your website. The research doesn't stop there. Your prospects also want to know if your organization's people are credible as well. And you are at the top of the list.

You can make an impression on prospects by establishing your own narrative with a

strong online presence. It's key for you to focus on consistent messaging as you build your credibility. Your statements and articles on sites like LinkedIn and during presentations must support the company mission. The content you provide must also demonstrate your proven expertise.

Your credibility outside the company impacts your credibility inside the company.

Much like your customers, your employees judge you by whether you seem to know what you are talking about and whether you will help them achieve their professional goals.

Employees read and watch what you say publicly. If they don't perceive what you say publicly as credible, they won't perceive you as credible in what you say internally.

Your digital credibility must be regularly monitored and managed. For a CEO, this includes:

- ✓ The leadership page of your company website
- ✓ Your LinkedIn profile
- ✓ How you appear when your name is searched on Google
- ✓ In press releases
- ✓ In the trade press
- ✓ On media and podcast interviews
- ✓ In databases like Zoominfo, SalesIntel, etc.
- ✓ On recorded keynotes and panel discussions

✓ On social media
✓ In online video
✓ On your investor website, if you have one
✓ Employee ratings and reviews
✓ Customer ratings and reviews

Your statements online, in the media and on stage must be consistent. You can't be caught saying one thing in public but saying a different thing to your employees. This is how credibility (and your ability to earn employee trust) is lost.

What you say must also be crystal clear. When leaders are ambiguous in their communications, direct reports will fill in the blanks with their own fears or gossip from others.

Effective leadership also hinges significantly on the congruence between what a leader says and what their company actually does. The leader's words set the tone for the entire organization. When there is a mismatch between what you say and what the company does, you undermine your credibility and your ability to be taken at face value next time.

Stakeholders rely on the leader's communications to make informed decisions. If the company's actions consistently contradict these communications, it erodes trust and can lead to a loss of confidence both internally and externally.

This loss of credibility can have far-reaching consequences, such as decreased investor confidence, loss of customer loyalty, a revenue decline, and a tarnished brand image. It also can adversely affect employee retention.

There is a compelling link between the leader's credibility and their employees' motivation.

I recently interviewed Jonathan Raymond, CEO of Refound, on the Manage Smarter podcast. He told me that "leaders can impact as much as 75% of an employee's performance." This impact can be seen in the level of employee motivation.

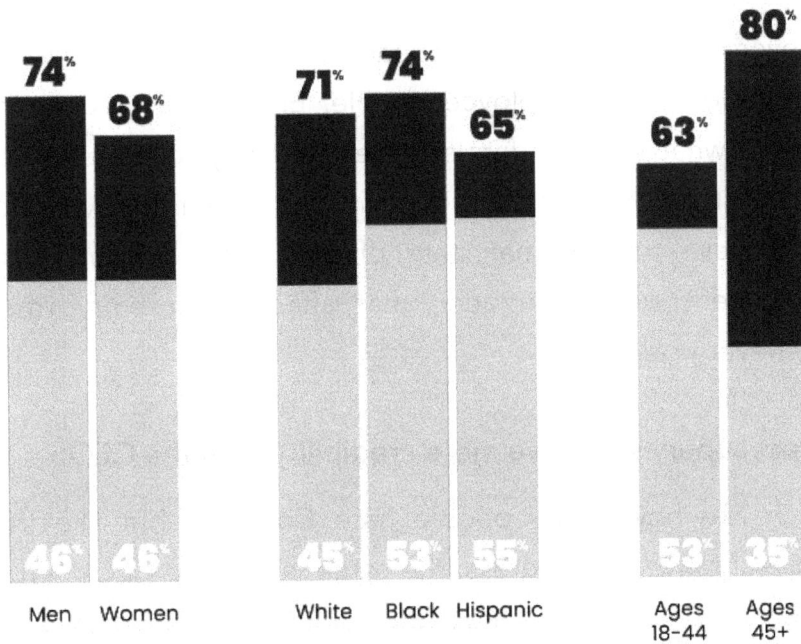

Chart data:
- Men: 74% / 46%
- Women: 68% / 46%
- White: 71% / 45%
- Black: 74% / 53%
- Hispanic: 65% / 55%
- Ages 18-44: 63% / 53%
- Ages 45+: 80% / 35%

■ "I have a credible CEO and feel motivated to do my best work."
▨ "I have a non-credible CEO and feel motivated to do my best work."

CEOs with high credibility are more likely to have employees who are motivated to do their very best at work every day. 68% of women and 74% of men who are motivated to do their best also believe their CEO is credible in what they say and do.

When the leader fosters a culture of trust and transparency, employees are more likely to feel secure in their roles, understand the company's vision and be motivated to contribute towards common goals.

In fact, nearly 3 out of 4 employees who are motivated at their jobs have a boss that "usually trusts them to do the right thing on their own."

Conversely, a disconnect can lead to confusion, demotivation and a decline in employee morale. Employees who cannot believe what their leaders say are less likely to be engaged, which can result in lower productivity and higher turnover rates. To achieve the optimal state of employee motivation, be transparent with information that affects their employment whenever possible.

Direct supervisors have more credibility than the CEO.

Much like how many people hate Congress but like their representative in Congress, the same is true for CEOs. When asked specifically about their CEO, only 54% of employees (not working for themselves) rank their CEO as credible in what they say and do. While it's much higher than the 26% for all CEOs, that number is hardly a ringing endorsement for company leadership.

But direct supervisors in the United States are **21%** more likely to be considered credible by workers 45+. They are **17%** more likely to be considered credible than their CEOs by younger workers (18-44).

To earn the kind of credibility scores your department heads enjoy, ensure that they are in lockstep with you (at least publicly).

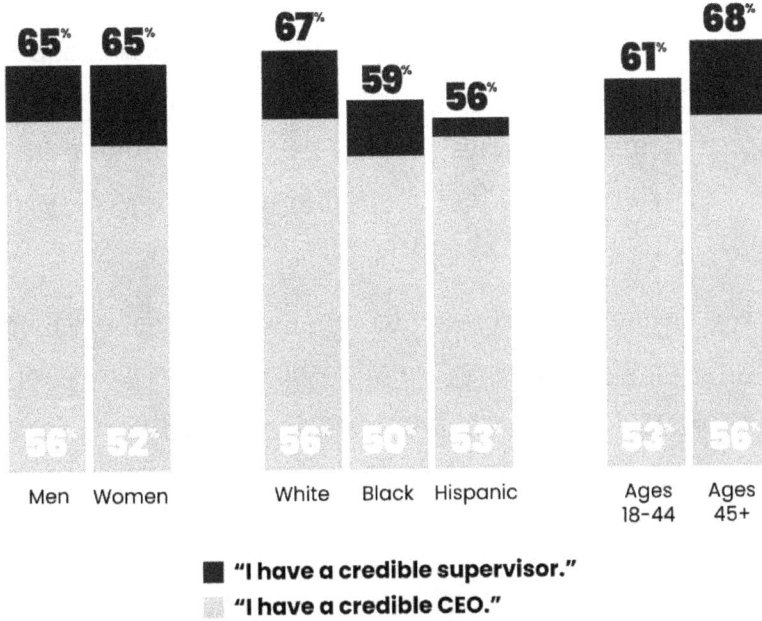

65% **65%** **67%** **59%** **56%** **61%** **68%**

56% **52%** **56%** **50%** **53%** **53%** **56%**

Men   Women   White   Black   Hispanic   Ages 18-44   Ages 45+

■ "I have a credible supervisor."
▨ "I have a credible CEO."

If there is a clear alignment between what you say and what the company does, your middle management finds it easier to make decisions and implement strategy that support your vision. They can lead their employees with confidence, knowing that their actions are supported by you and the rest of the leadership team.

The research backs this up. **71%** of employees with credible supervisors are motivated compared to **47%** with non-credible bosses.

However, inconsistencies between your words and actions can put department heads in a challenging position, as they struggle to justify actions and decisions to their teams, leading to inefficiencies and potential conflicts within departments.

Encourage your middle managers to provide respectful pushback in private if they disagree with one of your decisions before it is made. Always assume positive intent when they voice a concern. If they feel heard and taken seriously, you are more likely to be taken seriously.

Your willingness to listen to their concerns and ideas strengthens your working relationship. When your middle managers perceive you as being trustworthy, they'll feel safe about telling the truth, even if it may conflict with your vision for the organization.

When senior executives appear to be anxious, employees notice. They'll be anxious as well. When a leader is not authentic, or as transparent as the situation allows, employees sense they're not getting the full story. But when employees see a unified leadership and management team, they will be more likely to buy into the corporate mission.

Your credibility impacts the usefulness of employee feedback.

Whether there is an issue with a new product or service or the desire to sound the alarm about what a competitor is doing, information matters. In the long run, having the right data at the right time can mean the difference between being a market leader and missing the boat.

While your employees may believe in the corporate mission, they are closest to the work and more likely to notice a problem. Leaders should strive to build a workplace where all employees feel secure in pointing out potential problems and concerns. That's one reason why you have all those one-on-one meetings and employee engagement surveys. But none of that works if the employee doesn't feel psychologically safe to tell you the truth.

You have the power to fix that issue. The research reveals that the level of workplace safety an employee feels is linked to their leader's credibility.

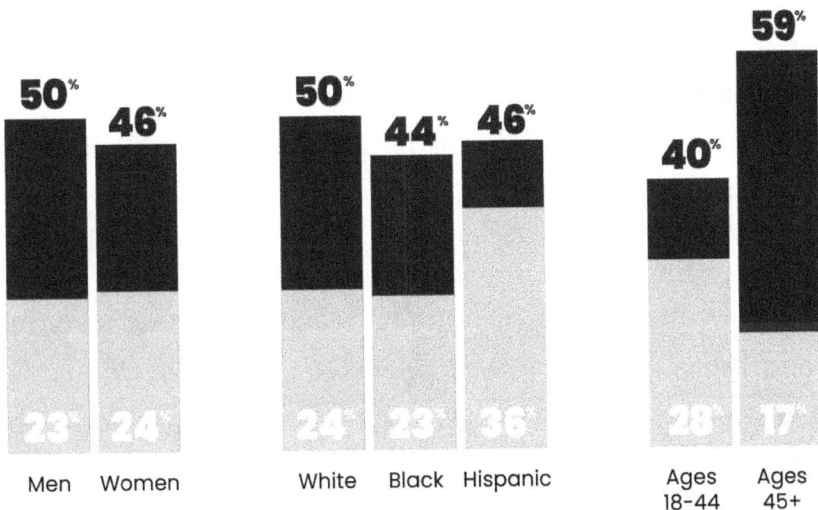

	Men	Women		White	Black	Hispanic		Ages 18-44	Ages 45+
Credible CEO	50%	46%		50%	44%	46%		40%	59%
Non-credible CEO	23%	24%		24%	23%	36%		28%	17%

■ "I have a credible CEO and feel safe to speak the truth at work."

"I have a non-credible CEO and feel safe to speak the truth at work."

Younger employees (60%) are 15% less likely to say they are motivated to do their best every day than older employees (69%). In addition, only 37% of younger employees feel they can safely speak the truth at work. For older workers, that number is 25% higher, standing at 46%.

However, senior leaders who have made credibility a priority in their organizations benefit from a positive trend. When they believe their CEOs are credible, 63% of younger employees try to do their best every day. And 40% feel safe when speaking the truth.

Meanwhile, 80% of older workers who say their CEO is credible are working hard every day and 59% feel safe about speaking the truth.

Summary

In an era when so many businesses and business leaders are under scrutiny, you cannot afford to come up short on credibility. Our full access, always-on economy allows your stakeholders and your competitors to capitalize on weakness.

Don't give them that opportunity. Maintaining credibility may sound like a full-time job. It is, and it is an effort you should move to the top of your list. Your efforts to transform your organization will pay off in terms of improved reputation, increased profitability and an enviable culture.

Scan the QR code to listen to my interview on
"C-Suite Success with Tricia Benn."

About the Author

C. Lee Smith

C. Lee Smith is the Global Sales Credibility Authority. He is recognized as one of the world's Leading Sales Consultants by *Selling Power* and as an Industry Leader by *Sales and Marketing Management* magazine. Lee is dedicated to empowering top executives to amplify their influence both within their organizations and in broader business arenas. As the founder and CEO of SalesFuel® and a Certified Behavioral Analyst, Lee specializes in transforming leadership approaches through deep behavioral insights.

He is the Amazon international bestselling author of *SalesCred: How Buyers Qualify Sellers* and *Hire Smarter, Sell More!*, as well as a regular contributor to *Entrepreneur* magazine. Through his innovative digital platforms, SalesCred® and TeamTrait™, he enhances leaders' credibility and provides strategic insights into job candidates before you interview them. Learn how Lee can help you accentuate authority, elevate your personal brand and meet revenue targets at cleesmith.com

Chapter Four

Putting People First in a World That Forgets

George Parente

The Foundation: Ethics and Integrity

When I think back on my own journey, the moments that shaped me most weren't about the numbers on the balance sheet or the accolades on the wall. They were about people-how I treated them, how I was treated, and the culture we built together. If there's a single thread that runs through every decision I make as a leader, it's this: Ethics and integrity are not just values; they are the foundation of trust, and trust is the currency of leadership. Ethics in an organization should always start at the top.

In today's business world, where headlines are filled with stories of leaders who lost their way, it's never been more critical to be the kind of person others can trust. Ethical leadership is a daily practice. It's not just about doing the right thing when others are watching; it's about doing the right thing, especially when they're not. It's about building a culture where every team member knows that integrity is non-negotiable, where taking responsibility is expected, and where accountability is the rule, not the exception.

I've learned that ethical leadership is a ripple effect. When leaders act with honesty, fairness, and transparency, those qualities cascade down through the organization. Teams become more cohesive, morale rises, job satisfaction increases, and performance improves. But it all starts at the top. As executives, we set the tone. Our actions-more than our words-define the culture.

I remind myself daily: every decision I make impacts not just our shareholders, but our stakeholders-our employees, our suppliers, our clients, the communities we serve, and the environment we inhabit. True hero leadership means considering the full weight of those decisions and never losing sight of the bigger picture.

Leading by Example: The CEO as Role Model

What sets exceptional CEOs apart? It's not just vision or charisma. It's the willingness to lead by example-to embody the values you want to see in your team.

I've always believed that non-verbal communication is more powerful than any memo or speech. People watch what you do far more closely than what you say. Early in my career, I realized that if I wanted to be taken seriously, I had to act seriously. That meant showing up every day with professionalism, positivity, and a focus on solutions-not problems.

One of my daily rituals is updating my voicemail to reflect where I am and when I'll be available. It might seem like a small thing, but it communicates respect for others' time and sets a standard for accountability. I update our shared office calendar and make sure every department has what they need before I dive into my own tasks. These rhythms, repeated day after day, create a culture of reliability and trust.

I recall a moment, years ago, when a potential buyer of DTG Consulting assumed I was the owner simply because of my presence and demeanor in a meeting. I didn't own a single share at the time. That experience drove home the point: people respond to how you carry yourself. If you want to be seen as a leader, you must consistently act like one.

Too often, people want the title and the promotion, but they don't realize that leadership is earned through actions, not words. If you want to be the hero in your organization, start by being the example others want to follow.

Communicating Vision: Clarity, Consistency, and Care

Shortly after stepping into the CEO role at DTG Consulting, I knew we needed a vision that was both clear and actionable. Our work is about people-clients, candidates, and colleagues. Our vision statement reflects that:

"To utilize our institutional knowledge for the betterment of our clients while finding the best career opportunities for our consultants."

This wasn't just a slogan. It was a commitment to put the client first, then the candidate, and finally, the individuals who make up DTG. That order matters. If we serve our clients well, we earn their trust and their business. If we help candidates find the right fit, we change lives-and those relationships often come full circle as former candidates become clients themselves. And if we do both of those things, we create opportunities for our own people.

Communicating this vision isn't a one-time event. It's a daily practice. It's woven into every meeting, every decision, every interaction. I make it a point to remind our team why we do what we do, and how each person contributes to that larger mission.

Exceptional leaders don't just talk about vision-they live it. They make sure everyone understands their role in achieving it. They celebrate wins, learn from setbacks, and keep the team focused on the bigger picture.

Transformational Leadership: Empowering Others to Lead

Before I became CEO, I spent 21 years as CFO at DTG. During that time, I watched talented people become stifled by a leadership style that was stuck in the past. Decisions were centralized, ideas were dismissed, and growth stagnated.

When I took the helm, I knew things had to change. I had studied transformational leadership, and I believed it was the only way forward. I didn't have all the answers-far from it. In fact, I had little practical experience in recruiting, account management, marketing, or IT. But I knew my team did.

So, I made a conscious choice: empower others to lead. I told my department heads, "This is where we need to go. How can you get us there?" I provided the tools and support they needed, but I stepped back and let them take ownership. I trusted them to make decisions, to innovate, to take risks.

The results were remarkable. People who had been stuck in a rut for years began to thrive. They brought fresh ideas, upgraded systems, and took the company to new heights. My lack of expertise in their areas became an asset--it forced me to listen, to trust, and to let go of control.

That's the essence of hero leadership: **it's not about being the smartest person in the room; it's about bringing out the best in others.** It's about creating a culture where everyone feels empowered to lead, to contribute, and to grow.

The Golden Rule of Leadership: Lead Others as You Wish to Be Led

If there's one principle that guides everything I do, it's this: Be the leader you wish you had. The golden rule of business is simple-lead others the way you would want to be led.

Throughout my career, I've experienced my share of poor management-leaders who ruled by fear, manipulation, or indifference. Each time, I made a mental note: "One day, I'll do it differently." I've tried to create a culture at DTG that I would have wanted early in my career-a culture of respect, empathy, and support.

That means putting myself in my team's shoes. I consider their workloads, their family responsibilities, their personal challenges. I worry about burnout. I know what that is like, as early in my career I worked in departments where the supervisors delegated a burdensome workload to their subordinates. Additionally, I took on as much work as I could, and then some, to make the impression on management that I was a valued employee to the organization. I check in, not just about work, but about life. I want every person on my team to feel seen, heard, and valued.

Take the Director of Human Resources, a Millennial who juggles her work and family obligations with grace and grit. Or the Director of Recruiting, who spent years trying to improve the recruiting department, only to have his ideas dismissed by a management team that may not have valued the opinion of someone with many decades less experience. My mission is to make sure people know how much they matter. That's what people-first leadership is all about.

The best leaders never forget where they came from. They remember what it felt like to be overlooked, undervalued, or misunderstood. They lead with empathy, humility, and a commitment to making things better for those who follow.

The Hero Leader's Legacy: Building a People-First Culture

At the end of the day, leadership isn't about titles or power. It's about impact. It's about leaving things better than you found them. It's about building a culture where people thrive, where trust is the norm, and where everyone feels empowered to be their best.

Hero leaders don't seek the spotlight-they shine it on others. They create environments where people are inspired to grow, to lead, and to make a difference. They understand that success is a team sport, and that the true measure of a leader is the legacy they leave behind.

So, if you want to be a hero leader-if you want to build a people-first organization-start with ethics and integrity. Lead by example. Being the leader we wished we would have had is one of driving motivations that allows us to lead others as though we are walking in their shoes. It's seeing a team member's present situation, doing some personal reflection, and thinking about how we would like to be treated if we were in their position. One of the reasons leaders struggle to lead in the shoes of those on their team is because they have a short memory. They forget those times they were treated poorly and how an inconsiderate boss made them feel. But strong leaders never forget where they have come from and lead their teams from a position of empathy and understanding.

Communicate your vision with clarity and consistency. Empower others to lead. And above all, treat people the way you wish you had been treated.

That's how you build trust. That's how you create lasting impact. And that's how you become the kind of leader the world needs now more than ever.

Scan the QR code to listen to my interview on "C-Suite Success with Tricia Benn."

About the Author

George Parente

In October 2021, after 21 years of working as the CFO of DTG Consulting Solutions, I became only the second CEO in the company's 49 years of operations. As CEO, I am responsible for overseeing all business operations at DTG. I am also still CFO of DTG and I manage the financial operations including banking and borrowing relations, budgeting and forecasting, financial statement preparation, payroll, and cost analysis. I have over 35 years of experience in the Accounting and Finance fields. I currently hold an active CPA license in New Jersey and Maryland. I have received dual Masters' degrees in Accounting and Business Administration. In connection with my Doctoral studies, I received a certification in Advanced Graduate Studies in Business Administration. In 2019, I obtained a certification in Negotiation Mastery from Harvard Business School. I also hold certifications in Business Law, Change Management, Sales Growth Strategies, and Business Contracts from Cornell University.

In 2023, Forbes Advantage Media published my book, In Their Shoes: Lessons On Corporate Leadership From A Former Uninspired Employee. My book became an Amazon best seller in the categories of Business Coaching and Mentoring (Kindle), and Business Management (Kindle). And it was the third best-selling hardcover book in Business Coaching and Mentoring.

I reside in Paramus, New Jersey with my wife of 16 years and our 14 year old twins, Daniela and Antonio. When I am not in the office, I love spending time with my wife and supporting our kids' hobbies. My daughter studies theater and we love going to plays in New York City. My son plays ice hockey, and I never miss one of his games. I am an avid fitness fanatic and try to exercise daily. Five years ago during the quarantine due to the Covid-19 Pandemic, I became reacquainted with my love of playing classical guitar, which I had given up to study business 35 years earlier. I am slowly relearning some of the pieces that were so important to me in my teen years.

LinkedIn: https://www.linkedin.com/in/george-parente/

Chapter Five

Leading with Heart: How I've Built a Culture of Shared Success

Jeff Meshey

When people ask me what it means to be a hero leader, I don't immediately think of myself in that light. I think of the people I work with every day, the community we serve, and the long tradition we've honored since Desert Financial Credit Union was founded back in 1939 by a group of teachers who pooled together $78.75 to help one another. That spirit of giving, of growing, of doing the right thing because it's right, that is what drives me.

Today, Desert Financial is an $9 billion institution serving over 475,000 members, but those numbers don't define our success. Our success is measured by our impact. Are we helping people? Are we creating opportunities? Are we making Arizona a better place to live, work, and thrive?

That's what matters most to me.

The Values That Define Us

Our culture at Desert Financial didn't happen by accident. We built it with purpose and clarity. The values that guide us—Personal Drive, Passion to Help, Big Thinking, Team Mindset, and Change Readiness—are more than just slogans. They're commitments we each make every single day.

I want everyone who works here, and everyone who does business with us, to feel like they matter. That's what our culture is built on. We're not just showing up to do a job; we're here to make a difference.

And to do that, we must think bigger. I often say that if you're not growing, you're dying. My predecessors were content to stay in a niche and maintain the status quo, but I knew we had the potential to reach more people, serve the greater good, and create more value for our members. Thinking big saved us and it's propelled us into a future I believe our founders would be proud of.

Giving Comes First

People sometimes ask how we can afford to give so much away. My answer is always the same—we budget for it first. Before anything else, we determine how much we're going to give back to our members, our communities, and, of course, our employees.

I'll never forget the early days of COVID. No playbook existed for how to lead during a global pandemic, but we knew people needed help—and fast. So, I recorded a message. No frills. Just me on camera, talking directly to our community. We restructured loans, created special hours for seniors, stocked essential supplies like toilet paper in our branches, and doubled down on giving.

We didn't do it for the attention. We did it because it was the right thing to do. But people noticed. And the relationships that were formed during that time have become some of our strongest to this day. Those relationships built during an incredibly difficult period withstood the test of time and endured.

One moment that stands out from that period is when we stepped in to support small businesses with PPP loans. Big banks struggled to meet the need. We stepped in quickly, and many of those small and medium-sized businesses are still with us because of it. That wasn't just about doing good—it was good business, too.

Aligning Growth with People

I've always believed that relationships are what drive our success. That's why we put a lot of energy into making sure that as Desert Financial grows, our people grow too.

We have team and individual incentives, sure—but the real alignment comes from the deeper investment we make in each person's future. One of the initiatives I'm most proud of is our InvestEd program. We partnered with Arizona State University, so every employee has the opportunity to take online classes or earn degrees completely free of charge. There are no strings attached—they can study whatever they want.

A lot of people told me it was crazy. "What if they leave?" they asked. My response? "What if they stay and grow?"

I believe that more educated people make better employees—and better people. And seeing our employees walk across the stage at our annual celebrations, degrees in hand, confirms that we're doing something truly meaningful and impactful. That program has improved our retention, helped with recruitment, and most importantly, it has changed lives.

Supporting Our Team from the Inside Out

Leadership means knowing when to carry the load and when to share it. As our organization continues to grow, I've leaned more into the power of succession planning and team support. We share responsibility among the executive team, not only to avoid burnout, but because collaboration makes us stronger.

During the pandemic, we also created an employee resource group called Mental Wellness Advocates. It was born out of our DEIA efforts, and it's become a vital support system for our staff. Mental health isn't something we ignore but something we invest in, openly and without stigma.

When people feel safe and supported, they perform at their best. That's good for them, and it's good for the business.

Communication Builds Trust

One thing I've learned is that in times of uncertainty, people need clarity and honesty. We're constantly looking for ways to communicate transparently with our team.

We use several tools: our internal intranet (which we call The Union), my own CEO Corner, strategy podcasts, regular Town Hall meetings, and employee surveys. We're not perfect, and we always want feedback on ways we can improve our communications, but we keep the conversation open.

When employees trust their leadership team, they stay. They care. They become part of something bigger than themselves.

A Story That Changed Me

In every leader's journey there is a defining moment that stands out from the rest. For me, it came early in my role as CEO when a long-time employee needed a kidney and asked for our help.

I was advised not to get involved by our legal and HR teams. It was 'too risky, too much liability.' But I couldn't ignore the human side of the situation. I said, "We're doing it." My team pushed back, warning me that we'd have to do it for anyone who asked in the future. I said, "Fine."

In the end, the donor wasn't even an employee. It was a member—someone who so deeply believed in who we are and what we stand for that she stepped up to donate her kidney. That moment captured everything we strive to be. It's hard to imagine a traditional bank having that kind of connection with its customers. But for us, it made perfect sense.

The lesson? Always do what you believe is right. That's where hero leadership begins. In fact, doing the right thing is what truly *defines* hero leadership.

Creating a Legacy of Disruption

We didn't start giving when the pandemic hit. We've been building a foundation of philanthropy for years. Today, we're one of the top 10 philanthropic organizations in Phoenix. And the work we do with Phoenix Children's Hospital is something I'll always be proud of—especially the "1 Darn Cool School," which helps kids keep up with their education while receiving treatment.

The first time I had to take my own daughter to that hospital, I felt a deep sense of reassurance—not just as a parent, but as a leader. I knew we were supporting a place that would take care of her, just like it's taken care of so many others.

To me, that's what legacy looks like. Real, lasting impact.

Thinking Bigger—Always

I still remember what it was like 30 years ago when I started here. Nobody really knew who we were. Today, when I ask people what they think of Desert Financial, the response is overwhelmingly positive. That didn't happen by accident or in the blink of an eye. It happened because we thought bigger, cared deeper, and stayed true to our mission: to share success.

Every other Monday, we welcome our new hires. When we ask why they joined, the response over and over is, "Because of what you're doing in the community." That's how I know we're on the right path.

Hero leadership isn't about grand gestures or dramatic speeches. It's about showing up every day with integrity, with vision, and with compassion. It's about helping people, standing by your values, and believing that businesses can—and should—do good. It's about doing what's right when no one is looking.

One of the things I'm most proud of is that many of my team, our members, and our business and community partners have acknowledged how genuine my interactions with them are. I try hard to really be present when these opportunities arise.

If I've learned anything in this journey, it's this: when you lead with heart, everything else follows.

Scan the QR code to listen to my interview on
"C-Suite Success with Tricia Benn."

About the Author

Jeff Meshey

Jeff Meshey is the President & CEO of Desert Financial Credit Union – a $9 billion, full-service Arizona based financial institution founded in 1939 with nearly 50 branches throughout Maricopa, Pinal, Coconino, Yavapai and Gila counties.

Mr. Meshey has been with Desert Financial since 1994. He has a broad background in the financial services industry with experience working for commercial banks, savings banks and credit unions. He became CEO of Desert Financial in 2017.

During his tenure at Desert Financial, the institution's total assets have grown more than twelvefold, rebranded, converted to a community charter and expanded the branch network significantly. Desert Financial is frequently voted the best credit union in Arizona, one of the Best Places to Work in Phoenix and is a past winner of the Better Business Bureau's Torch Award for Ethics. In the past few years, Desert Financial has been recognized by Forbes, Newsweek and JD Power as being a top credit union in Arizona.

Mr. Meshey and his wife Debbie reside in Chandler and are actively involved in the community. He was recognized by AZ

Big Media as an Arizona Business Leader in 2024 and as a Phoenix Titan 100 in 2023 and 2024 and he is a member of Greater Phoenix Leadership. He also is the Chair Elect of the Board of the Phoenix Chapter of the American Heart Association and was recognized as their Executive Volunteer of the Year in 2023.

LinkedIn: https://www.linkedin.com/in/jeffmeshey/

Chapter Six

Wealth, Wisdom, and Stewardship in Leadership

Larry Pendleton

Hero leadership isn't always found in the boardroom spotlight or behind a startup's flashy pitch deck. Sometimes, it's in the quiet discipline of stewardship—the kind that understands wealth is not just about accumulation, but about what you do with it. My journey as a CPA, investor, and CEO has taught me this: leading a business heroically means bringing value to others and building something that outlives you.

I've spent nearly two decades immersed in tax strategy, financial planning, and real estate investing. But my roots run deeper than numbers. They run into the foundation of purpose. My partner, Terreon Conyers, and I started PC Financial Services because I believed there was a better way to help people—not just to pay less in taxes, but to achieve financial freedom. To think generationally. To become investors, not just earners.

Over the years, I've helped thousands of investors save thousands of dollars. But the money saved is only a means to something greater: freedom. When you free people financially, you also unlock their creativity, their confidence, their courage. That's where hero leadership begins.

Building with Vision and Discipline

For me, the hero's journey in leadership begins with clarity of vision and the discipline to follow through. I've learned that success isn't just about seeing opportunities—it's about stewarding them. It's about setting a standard that demands consistency and focus even when the numbers are tough, the market is uncertain, and the pressure mounts.

In my company, we don't make promises we can't back with numbers. We educate investors to understand why certain strategies may or may not work for them. I often tell my clients, "Don't let the tax tail wag the dog." Whether we're structuring a cost segregation study or 1031 exchange, the aim is always the same: build a foundation that endures.

When I look at leadership, I don't just think about what I can do—I think about what I can teach. The true test of leadership is whether others can rise because of your presence. I don't have employees because I want to encourage the people I work with to build a foundation and work environment that is suitable for them. That includes putting them in situations where they may need to hire employees or bring on contractors themselves. As they build their business, we have open discussions of how their people are developing and I can share my experiences of overseeing people to see if it would be helpful to them.

Hero leaders multiply impact by multiplying leaders.

The Mindset of Stewardship

One of the most overlooked qualities in leadership is stewardship. It's not flashy, but it's foundational. Stewardship is understanding that everything you lead—your business, your wealth, your influence—isn't just for your benefit. It's a trust. A responsibility.

This mindset changes how you approach everything. It shapes how you treat your team, how you serve your clients, how you give back to your community. I serve on nonprofit boards and the city's planning commission not because it boosts my profile, but because I believe in modeling investment in people and place. When you give back, you remind yourself that success is never solely yours—it's a resource to be shared.

Stewardship also means knowing when to step forward and when to step back. In real estate, I've done it all—notes, rentals, syndications, short-term rentals, new construction. But the lesson isn't in the variety—it's in the discernment. A hero leader doesn't chase every opportunity. He or she chooses the right ones. Not just the ones with returns, but the ones with resonance.

Resilience Built Through Experience

The market doesn't care how many hours you worked or how confident you felt. It responds to data. So does leadership. That's why experience is everything. I didn't become a hero leader because I never failed—I became one because I learned how to turn setbacks into stepping stones.

I've been through deals that fell apart and clients who disappeared. I've watched the economy tighten and interest rates surge. But I never let the storm define my outcome. What defines us is how we respond. Do we pivot? Do we protect what matters most? Do we press forward with wisdom?

I tell younger professionals this all the time: hero leadership is quiet. It's not always public. Sometimes, it's you alone at your desk at 2 a.m. reconciling a mess that no one else saw coming. Sometimes it's owning a mistake, correcting it, and protecting your client's trust. That's leadership that lasts. That's leadership that leaves a legacy.

And let's be clear: resilience isn't just bouncing back—it's bouncing forward. It's not about returning to what was. It's about moving toward something better. I've learned that failure doesn't define you unless you let it. What defines you is your capacity to get back up, refine your approach, and lead with renewed clarity.

Teaching People to Think Differently About Money

The work we do at PC Financial Services goes beyond taxes. We teach people to see wealth differently. Most people are working to pay bills. We want to flip that mindset—we want them working to build legacy.

That means educating on the power of passive income. We introduce investors to options like private lending secured by real estate, syndications, and mortgage note investing. Every conversation is about teaching financial literacy at a level that leads to action.

We often overlook just how transformational financial knowledge can be. It's not just about balance sheets—it's about belief systems. When someone realizes they don't have to live paycheck to paycheck, when they see a path to financial stability and freedom, their whole posture changes. They walk taller. They make decisions with confidence. They become better leaders in their homes, their communities, and their careers.

The hero leader's role isn't to hold all the answers. It's to create a culture where people start asking better questions. It's to help them think differently, plan differently, act differently. Because when people start to shift how they think about money, they start to shift how they think about life.

Leading With Integrity in a Profit-Driven World

Integrity still matters. In fact, in a world obsessed with speed and scale, integrity is the differentiator. At PC Financial Services, we don't chase volume at the expense of value. We don't promise quick fixes. We chase relationships. We add value by educating and making recommendations based on the numbers.

Why? Because leadership is built on trust, and trust is built on truth. I've turned down deals that didn't align with our values. I've walked away from clients who refused transparency. That's not loss—that's legacy. When you lead with integrity, you attract people who value the same. You build a business that doesn't just make money—it makes a mark.

And yes, the pressure to grow fast is real. But I believe that if we build slowly and build right, we build something that lasts. That's hero leadership. It's not chasing scale for its own sake— it's scaling with substance.

Purpose Beyond Profit

Everything I do—every tax strategy, every investor conversation, every board I serve on—is driven by a deeper purpose. I want to help people create wealth not just for themselves, but for their communities, their churches, their children.

That's why financial stewardship matters. Because when people build well, they give well. They serve well. They lead well. And that's how you create a ripple effect that changes cities and generations.

I didn't get into business just to count dollars. I got into business to build bridges. I want the next generation to see that success isn't just for the privileged—it's for the prepared. It's for the ones who are willing to learn, to sacrifice, and to lead.

We often talk about return on investment. But what about return on influence? What about the lives you impact, the communities you strengthen, the systems you improve? Those are the metrics that matter most in the long run. That's the kind of wealth worth building.

Final Thoughts: Becoming the Hero You Needed

When I think about hero leadership, I think about the mentors who spoke life into me when I was just getting started. I think about the partners that supported me along the way. I think about the mistakes I made and the grace I was given. And I think about the responsibility I now carry—to be that kind of hero for someone else.

A hero leader doesn't just solve problems—they sow seeds. They invest in people so the people will also invest in themselves. They plan with precision and lead with heart. They understand that legacy isn't what you leave behind—it's who you lift while you're here.

So, whether you're leading a business, building your brand, or just starting your journey, remember this: Hero leadership isn't about titles. It's about impact. It's about consistency. It's about character.

Lead with wisdom. Lead with purpose. Lead like a steward. And never forget—the most heroic thing you can do as a leader is help someone else believe they can build, too.

Scan the QR code to listen to my interview on

"C-Suite Success with Tricia Benn."

About the Author

Larry Pendleton

As The Investor's CPA℠, my mission is to help fellow investors achieve financial abundance by increasing their passive income secured by real estate and reducing their taxes with effective tax strategies.

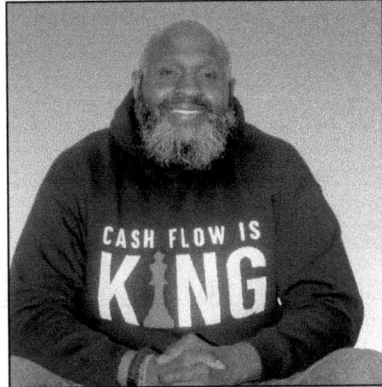

I have been a CPA and tax strategist for around two decades with a focus on tax strategies for investors. My company, PC Financial Services, has helped thousands of investors across the US with tax planning to save them thousands of dollars in taxes. Along with tax consulting, we add value with cost segregation studies, accredited investor validation, and tax preparation.

I have also been a real estate investor for over a decade. I have been an active participant in various ventures across the US consisting of; mortgage notes, multi & single family rentals, syndications, corporate housing, short-term rentals, new development, and flips. Besides the current portfolio of notes, rentals, and new construction, our focus now is educating investors on how to achieve greater returns than their bank or retirement accounts, secured by real estate by being private lenders.

I serve on various Boards of nonprofits that promote the development of the youth and my community. I also serve on the Planning Commission for the city of Norfolk, VA.

Most importantly, I am married to my extraordinary wife, Whitney, and the proud father of our 2 sons, Larry III and Wesley.

Social:
LinkedIn: https://www.linkedin.com/in/larry-pendleton-jr-cpa-msa-493aa249/
Facebook:
https://www.facebook.com/profile.php?id=100012395678547

Chapter Seven

Leading from the Inside Out:
The Heroic Charge of Energy, Empathy, and AI-Powered Execution

Mark L. Madrid

To lead today is to redefine what power means. It is no longer about top-down control. It is about bottom-up conviction. Leadership is no longer about titles. It is about results-driven transformation. And this transformation starts with energy.

As CEO and Founder of Breakthrough Mavens, I lead from the inside out. Every day, I show up with three non-negotiables: energy, discipline, and grit. These signature ingredients with authentic empathy fuel execution. This is our model and our mantra. And it works. Because in an era saturated with noise, the rarest currency is clarity.

"The quality of a leader is reflected in the standards they set for themselves." -Ray Kroc

At Breakthrough Mavens, we do not just counsel businesses. We activate people. We do not just scale operations. We scale belief. I launched this firm not only as a pivot, but also as a personal renaissance. It was a reckoning that entrepreneurship did not have to mean suffering; that executives could drive profit without burning out; that purpose and profit are not in conflict but in covenant.

Energy as the Ultimate Differentiator

Energy is everything. It is the tone-setter. The culture-builder. The will-starter. When you walk into a room with energy rooted in purpose, people listen.

I served at the highest levels of corporate America, government, and civic service. I have counseled billion-dollar ventures. Equally important, I have walked with founders whose lights were dimming until someone re-lit their belief. That someone was me. And that is why Breakthrough Mavens exists.

We are a battle-tested boutique firm built to breathe more energy into scaling companies and determined individuals. We fuse blue-collar grit with white-collar experience. We combine C-suite savvy with empathetic and relatable soul. And increasingly, we do this by integrating AI and AGI to unlock breakthrough imagination, innovation, and productivity. Furthermore, we save precious time that can be devoted to family, dear friends, and personal causes.

AI and AGI: Amplifying, Not Replacing Humanity

Let me be clear: AI is not a threat; it is a tool. And when used ethically, it does not erase human value, it amplifies it.

At Breakthrough Mavens, we deploy AI and even early AGI principles to take the friction out of growth; to protect founders from burnout; to make data-driven decisions with human-centered outcomes. We train our clients to think and imagine with AI, not to fear it.

In fact, I collaborated with author and award-winning economic developer Kevin Johns on national guidebooks on leveraging AI to elevate entrepreneurial excellence, create kid economics and eliminate homelessness. Why? If not now, then when? If not us, then who?

Leadership by Example, Not Popularity

"Let us remember the Golden Rule: 'Do unto others as you would have them do unto you' (Matthew 7:12) ... The yardstick we use for others will be the yardstick which time will use for us." -Pope Francis

My parents were my first CEOs. With unrelenting grit, resourcefulness, and conviction, they ran our family's welding business with bare hands and full hearts. Dad and mom never asked for applause and yet churned consistent results. Their lessons followed me from the farming community to Wall Street to the White House to Main Street.

Also, they taught me that empathy is not softness, it is strategy. It fuels loyalty, inspires innovation, and translates directly into profitability. That is not theory, it is lived experience.

Well-Being Is a KPI

I do not lead from a mountaintop. I lead in the trenches. My check-ins with my team are not just about metrics, they are about meaning. A walk-and-talk. An actual phone call. An authentic smile. These are the small things that energize culture.

Every early morning, I practice discipline: Shaun T's T25 workouts (on BODi), prayer, and productivity rituals. Why? Because if I am not centered, how can I be present for our people?

"People don't care how much you know until they know how much you care." -Theodore Roosevelt

Presence is my superpower. And presence unlocks performance. "You are everywhere." Yes, I am.

The Risk That Became a Reckoning

Transitioning from 31 years of unbelievably rewarding positions and a lifetime of overcoming tragedies, it was time to be my own boss...all the time. Jubilantly, I launched Breakthrough Mavens. This was not a risk; it was a reckoning of will and purpose. I had no investors. Just credit cards, conviction, and a soul-deep belief that it was time to honor God's assignment, to fuel excellence in others. I leaned on faith, on *ganas* (grit in Spanish), on the blue-collar DNA gifted to me by my parents, and on my signature energy, discipline, and grit.

"Hardships often prepare ordinary people for an extraordinary destiny." -C.S. Lewis

That destiny is Breakthrough Mavens and my #LivingLegacy of teaching *Self-Fueling Excellence*. Now, we fight for energy over exhaustion; for strategy over chaos; for humans over hollow systems.

We stand at the intersection of technology, trust, and results-driven transformation. And we are winning, for our clients and their bottom lines.

Competing With Conviction

I do not just love to compete. I live to compete. And, unapologetically, I play to win.

Since second grade, when I won my first county spelling bee, I have been wired to pursue excellence with fierce conviction. Whether I was competing in running, climbing corporate ladders, or navigating boardrooms, I have carried the same mantra: Play by the rules; outlast the noise; and win with integrity, energy, discipline, and grit.

I have won competitive races and closed high-stakes deals. What never changes? The conviction to be my best and to help others find their best. My faith in God, my steel tenacity, and my relentless energy keep me grounded. And grounded leaders rise highest.

I compete with joy. I compete with compassion. And I always compete with purpose.

People Over Process. Profit Through Purpose.

Here is what I have learned: when you pour into people, they pour into performance.

Empathy? It is good ethics and good economics. Retention. Culture. Brand reputation. Innovation. These are not soft stats; they are the bedrock of profitability in today's rapidly evolving economy.

And when we integrate AI into business culture—with care, clarity, and compliance—what we unlock is exponential. Less burnout. Faster insights. Elevated combined intelligence. And yes, profitability.

"Purpose and profit are not in conflict. They are in covenant." - Mark L. Madrid

Hero Leadership in Action

What is a real hero moment?

It is not just the standing ovations or the stage. It is the whisper in a hallway when someone says, "You helped me believe again." It is the founder who wanted to quit—but did not. It is the emerging leader who stepped up because you made room.

This is impact. This is influence. This is leadership.

Legacy Reimagined

The legacy I chase is not biography headlines. It is lives impacted.

It is companies made whole. Cultures made magnetic. And a future made possible by energy, empathy, and execution in harmony.

We are pioneering a new model of executive leadership: the Chief Energy Officer.

Because the most effective CEOs of the future will not just drive profit. They will generate contagious energy. They will be culture-chargers, clarity-makers, and breakthrough-builders. That is the blueprint we are building now at Breakthrough Mavens.

The Hero Charge

To every founder, CEO, and leader reading this: you do not need to wear a cape. You just need to answer the call.

To lead from the inside out. To put presence above performance. To embed AI and innovation in ways that advance the human spirit, not erase it. To be as focused on who you build as what you build.

Because that is how the world should shift, not in sweeping declarations, but in one breakthrough at a time.

This is the good battlefield. And I am honored to show up for it prepared, energetic and full of hope and ready to win—every single day.

I submit for your consideration:

- Energy is not optional, it is the oxygen of modern leadership.
- AI is not replacing us; it is revealing us.
- Purpose is not a brand message, it is a performance multiplier.
- Compete with conviction. Lead with heart. Win with empathy.
- We are not here to make noise. We are here to replace it.
- Legacy is not built in headlines. It is built on how you made people feel without the spotlight.
- Do not wear a cape. Wear conviction.
- We are not just scaling companies. We are scaling belief.
- ENERGY is everything. Believe in yourself. Never give up. Life is a gift.

Scan the QR code to listen to my interview on
"C-Suite Success with Tricia Benn."

About the Author

Mark L. Madrid

"I've been taught to be an elephant, not a hippo. Elephants have big ears, while hippos have small ones. The most important questions I ask are, how are you doing, and what does success look like for you?" -Mark L. Madrid

Mark L. Madrid, CEO and founder of Breakthrough Mavens, LLC, serves corporate America, small business owners, senior executives, boards, and nonprofits in a collaborative and energizing setting. As an in-demand, dynamic keynote speaker and new author, he also appeals to large audiences at the corporate level. Breakthrough Mavens, LLC, is a fractional C-Suite services form powered by AI and distinguished by customer experience and human interaction.

Currently, Mark has notable institutional fractional executive roles as Visiting Scholar at the Clinton School of Public Service at the University of Arkansas and Entrepreneur-In-Residence at the National Minority Supplier Development Council (NMSDC). He serves on the Board of Directors for the Texas State University McCoy College of Business Foundation, the Board of Advisors at Trez.co, the Advisory Council of the Hispanic

Wealth Project and the Executive Board of Directors of FRIENDS, Friends of the American Latino Museum, a national advocacy campaign striving for the creation of a Smithsonian National American Latino Museum. Additionally, Mark is a proud member of C-SUITE NETWORK™ and The Hero Club, an invite-only organization for Founders, CEOs, and Investors with the vision and drive to lead companies with distinguished integrity, transparency, and action.

Mark is the author of his first book, *Energy, 21 Uncomplicated & Easy Tips to Start Your Day Energized*, the first in a book series, *Self-Fueling Excellence*, Mark's unique story and experiences resonate with the American public. He attributes his success to energy, discipline, grit, perseverance, and hope—cornerstones he relies on and encourages his clients to utilize through his business, offering fractional C-Suite services and cyber/AI consulting services.

Mark grew up as part of a humble Texas Panhandle farming community, and his journey exemplifies the power of resilience and the pursuit of dreams against all odds. Raised by migrant farmworker parents, Mark saw firsthand the value of arduous work, and he learned about determination when they built a successful welding business from scratch. This early exposure to entrepreneurship laid the foundation for Mark's future.

A trailblazer, Mark became the first-ever Hispanic valedictorian in his town, earning a full scholarship to the University of Texas at Austin. This pivotal milestone led to his position with JP Morgan on Wall Street in 1994, and he continued through significant roles in corporate executive banking, nonprofit leadership, and public service.

He credits much of his tenacity and the ability to navigate the complexities of business and life to his father's resourcefulness and the memory of his brother, Leroy, who died unexpectedly at age five.

Professionally, Mark's accomplishments are extensive. He served as a Presidential Appointee and head official at the U.S. Small Business Administration, Mark's office supported millions of small businesses between 2021 and 2024. Prior to the SBA, Mark served as the CEO of the Stanford University Latino Entrepreneurship Initiative/Latino Business Action Network and President and CEO of the Greater Austin Hispanic Chamber (GAHCC). Under his direction the GAHCC was named the United States Hispanic Chamber of the Year by the United States Hispanic Chamber of Commerce.

Mark's passion, leadership, action, and results benefiting the U.S. small business ecosystem is nationally recognized as grounded, empathetic, and accessible. Today, Mark is harnessing the power of AI to advance inclusive economies, excellence frameworks, and innovation to uplift entrepreneurs. In so doing, he is consistently consulting with industry experts to ensure compliance with legal and ethical frameworks.

Mark was named the 2019 Silicon Valley Nonprofit CEO of the Year by the Silicon Valley Business Journal, and his impressive honors include his designation as an Honorary Colonel for the

United States Army Reserve, the Jefferson Award for public service, the American Airlines Extra Mile Award, the Courage in Government Award from the National Business Inclusion Consortium, and the Latino Leaders Maestro Award for his lifelong achievement for the economic prosperity of the U.S. Latino cohort.

His education credentials, a BBA with honors from UT Austin and a Master's in Nonprofit Administration with honors from the University of Notre Dame, further accentuate his academic achievements and dedication to continuous learning. Mark was awarded the Community Emerging Legacy Award by the University of Texas at Austin Division of Diversity and Community Engagement. The University of Notre Dame Mendoza College of Business named him the recipient of Mendoza's Alumni Service Award.

During the 2015 Notre Dame Mendoza College of Business Graduate Business Diploma Ceremony, Mark was honored with the Rev. Theodore M. Hesburgh, CSC Founder's Award, and the David J. LaBarre Community Service Award.

The Rev. Theodore M. Hesburgh, CSC Founder's Award is given to one University of Notre Dame Master of Nonprofit Administration (MNA) student who is highly-regarded by the University of Notre Dame Mendoza College of Business faculty, possesses the integrity and character consistent with Notre Dame and displays leadership and scholarship within the Mendoza College of Business.

The David J. LaBarre Community Service Award is given to one Master of Nonprofit Administration (MNA) student who is highly-regarded by his/her fellow MNA classmates, possesses the integrity and character consistent with Notre Dame, demonstrates a willingness to help other students and displays a commitment to both Notre Dame and surrounding communities.

For the University of Texas at Austin McCombs School of Business Centennial Celebration, Mark was one of 60 BBA alumni featured in a campaign celebrating the 80,000+ alumni. One of Mark's favorite expressions is "No one can ever take your education from you, so never stop learning."

Beyond his professional life, Mark treasures his faith, partner, family, and his pet, Champ. His love for competitive running reflects his lifelong love of discipline and self-improvement. Mark L. Madrid embodies the catchphrase "relentless pursuit of excellence and winning in the good battlefield," setting him apart nationally for business excellence, inspiration, and action.

LinkedIn: https://www.linkedin.com/in/markmadrid/

Chapter Eight

The Hero Leader's Way to Culture, Rapid Growth and Consistent Wins

Michael Brinker

There's a moment in every leader's journey where the mask of competence falls away, revealing what truly drives us: purpose. That moment came for me not in a boardroom or during a high-stakes negotiation, but in a simple conversation— one that forced me to reckon with the kind of leader I was becoming and the kind I needed to be. When your business is feeding more than 100 mouths and families every month, you ask yourself: How do we lead as heroes, not just operators?

Leading a business is often described in terms of metrics, margins, and market share. But hero leadership? That's a different archetype altogether. It's not about capes and accolades. It's about service. It's about clarity. It's about waking up every day and choosing excellence over perfection, kindness over toughness, and participation over attendance.

Finding Purpose in the Numbers

As a Chief Business and Finance officer, numbers are my terrain. I can tell you exactly how much liquidity we have, what our burn rate is, or how we're allocating capital across strategic initiatives. But if all I'm doing is optimizing spreadsheets, I've missed the point. Finance is a tool for mission—not the mission itself.

In a traditional environment, finance is about control and risk mitigation. In a purpose-driven business, it becomes about enablement. My role is to remove friction—financial, operational, and emotional—so others can do their best work. Encouraging to truly understand the relationship between outcomes and their causes, driving the mind towards challenging output with plausibility questions.

The hero leader doesn't hide behind Excel. They use it as a sword to cut through the noise, providing clarity so teams can act with conviction. We don't lead with opacity or jargon. We lead with understanding—because transparency builds trust, and trust compounds faster than any investment return.

The Power of Clarity

I often say that clarity is kindness. It's also power.

One of the greatest responsibilities of a hero leader is to create coherence in a chaotic world. People are bombarded with information, uncertainty, and competing priorities. When we're clear—about where we're going, why it matters, and how each person contributes—we unlock energy.

In my teams I practice what I call "earned clarity." It's not handed down from a mountain. It's forged in conversation, iteration, and shared ownership. We define outcomes before outputs. We make sure people understand the "why" behind the "what." And we don't just tolerate questions—we invite them. That's where alignment lives.

In meetings, I always ask, "Are we making this more complicated than it needs to be?" Simplicity isn't a lack of sophistication; it's a sign of mastery. When we strip away ego and complexity, we make room for momentum.

Building Cultures of Psychological Safety

You can't lead heroically if your team is afraid of speaking up.

Psychological safety is more than a buzzword. It's the air teams need to breathe. Without it, people shrink. With it, they soar. One of my key responsibilities is to cultivate an environment where even uncomfortable truths are welcomed, not punished. That means owning my mistakes in front of others. That means saying, "I don't know," without shame.

In the team cultures that I have built, we give each other the benefit of the doubt. We challenge ideas without attacking people. We assume positive intent, even when emotions run high.

And we don't weaponize perfection. The hero leader understands that vulnerability is a strength, not a liability. When I'm real, it gives others permission to be real, too. And that authenticity? It's rocket fuel for trust.

Most importantly, I don't hold back addressing the elephant in the room all the time. During my time on Wall Street, I learned that even the janitorial services knew how good the business was going. If there was a lot of paper to clean, there was a lot of business. If there wasn't, then sales were slow. As a hero leader, understand that your team knows more than you think about the business, so don't pretend things are greater than they are. Be real with the people what the reality looks like, and you will earn even greater loyalty.

Reimagining Performance and Success

For too long, performance has been measured by output alone. Revenue. KPIs. Efficiency. These matter, of course—but they're incomplete. Thriving towards excellence in work results and personal behavior is the foundation of progress.

Hero leadership requires us to redefine success. I measure not just what tasks get done, but what is the persons overall behavior within the team and company. We ask within the team: Are people thriving, not just collecting a paycheck? Are we truly understanding the dots between different work streams, not just ticking of To-do lists? Are we leaving people and systems better than we found them? Is a person's behavior within the team and company creating a great work environment, and not displaying toxic character traits?

I've seen firsthand how this shift in focus changes behavior. When success is tied to impact, not ego, people become more collaborative. More innovative. More resilient. And ironically, performance improves—because it's grounded in purpose, not pressure.

I remind my team often: You are not your output. You are not your title. You are not your inbox. You are a human being with intrinsic worth—and when we treat people that way, extraordinary things happen.

Scaling Trust Through Systems

Trust doesn't scale automatically. It has to be designed into the system.

In any fast-growing company, the risk is that alignment breaks down as complexity increases. Hero leaders anticipate this. They build frameworks that reinforce shared values, decision rights, and communication rhythms.

One of my proudest achievements has been architecting financial systems that don't just optimize dollars—they reinforce a culture of excellence. Allocate priorities and budgets based on mission goals, not political capital or textbook distribution. Conducting postmortems on major initiatives, even when they succeed, to foster learning. Decentralizing decision-making where possible, empowering teams to act quickly within guardrails.

Systems are not bureaucracy. When designed intentionally, they are expressions of trust. And when you pair strong systems with strong relationships, you get what I call "autonomy with accountability"—the holy grail of organizational performance.

The Gift of Feedback

Hero leaders don't wait for the annual review to speak the truth. We speak instantly.

Feedback is a gift—but only if it's delivered with care and received with humility. I teach my leaders and team members to frame feedback around impact, not intent. With high performers around me, they already know when they screwed up, I don't need to tell them I recognized a mistake. It's not about blame—it's about growth.

Personally, I've grown more from difficult feedback than any conference or book. The hardest truth I ever heard? That I was moving so fast I was creating confusion. That stung—but it was true. It helped me slow down, communicate more clearly, and listen more deeply.

The hero leader isn't the smartest person in the room. They're the one most open to evolving. Feedback isn't failure—it's fertilizer for development.

Leading with Conviction and Care

One of the paradoxes of hero leadership is balancing conviction with care.

We have to make tough calls. Say no. Set boundaries. Hold the line. But we can do so with empathy. With listening. With context. With kindness. Being decisive doesn't mean being harsh. And being compassionate doesn't mean being weak.

I've learned that the most enduring influence comes not from charisma, but consistency. When people know what to expect from you—how you'll respond, what you'll prioritize, how you'll treat them—they feel safe. And from that safety comes speed, creativity, and loyalty.

When those values are known, shared, and operationalized, leadership becomes less about control and more about orchestration. It becomes a symphony of trust, where each person plays a vital part.

The lived values I want to see in all my teams are 1) Thriving for excellence, not perfection 2) Leading by kindness, not toughness 3) Seeking participation, not attendance.

First Key to Growth: Keep Sales Close to the Chest

If you want to understand the soul of your business, step into a sales conversation. Hero leadership demands proximity to the customer—not just to their purchases, but to their pain. When we delegate sales too quickly or too far from the core, we don't just outsource a function — we lose sight of what makes people buy in the first place.

I've sat in rooms where sales figures looked strong on paper, yet the story behind them was hollow. Growth without connection is fragile. Keeping sales leadership internal means more than hitting quotas—it means living the values we preach, at the front lines and behind the curtain.

The hero leader doesn't chase volume blindly. They stay close to the why behind every yes. Sales isn't just about closing deals—it's about opening relationships. And those relationships are the lifeblood of lasting growth.

Second Key to Growth: Protect the Standard Relentlessly

There was a season when customer complaints blindsided me—honest feedback from good people who felt let down. It was a gut punch. And it taught me something vital: You cannot lead with excellence if your promises are slipping through the cracks.

Quality isn't something you inspect after the fact—it's something you weave into every process, every conversation, every touchpoint. Hero leaders don't rely on third-party validations or quarterly audits to tell them how they're doing. They trust their own senses—the feel of the product, the tone of the client call, the subtle signs of disengagement in a team member's eyes.

Great quality control is a lived practice. It's not a department—it's a mindset. And when you bring it close, when you walk the floor, ask the hard questions, and sweat the details, you build a brand that doesn't just sell—it earns trust.

Third Key to Growth: Know Your Numbers in Real-Time

Every founder dreams of the surge—that moment when revenue spikes, doors open, and momentum hits its stride. But with that dream comes danger: systems that buckle, discipline that frays, and decisions made in the rearview mirror.

Hero leaders don't fly blind. They don't wait 30 days for a financial report to tell them what already happened. They build systems that reflect reality as it unfolds—financial infrastructure that delivers insight within hours, not weeks.

In moments of rapid growth, you need clarity that cuts fast and deep. What products are driving margin? Where is cash bleeding out? What levers can be pulled today, not next quarter?

When finance is wired to inform, not just record, you stop reacting and start steering. And that's what hero leadership looks like: decisiveness powered by truth, not guesswork. Systems that speak quickly. People who listen carefully. And leaders who act with the confidence that only real-time clarity can bring.

Choosing Heroism Every Day

Hero leadership isn't a title or a trait. It's a choice—a daily one.

It's choosing to show up fully, even when you're tired. It's choosing to speak truth, even when it's uncomfortable. It's choosing to believe in people's potential, even when they haven't yet seen it themselves.

I don't always get it right. None of us do. But perfection isn't the point. Progress is. Progress is based on thriving for excellence. And every time we choose courage over convenience, clarity over chaos, and community over control, we inch closer to becoming the leaders our teams—and this world—deserve.

In this crucible of business, may we all choose to lead not just with skill, but with soul. Because the true hero doesn't seek the spotlight. They light the path.

Scan the QR code to listen to my interview on
"C-Suite Success with Tricia Benn."

About the Author

Michael Brinker

Architect of Scalable Growth, Strategic Finance, and Purpose-Driven Leadership

Michael Brinker is a global business and finance leader whose journey has crossed sectors, continents, and crises—yet remained anchored in a single, unwavering belief: that leadership is measured not only in outcomes, but in the systems and cultures we build to sustain them. With over 15 years of experience spanning high-growth startups, complex manufacturing operations, financial institutions, and government-affiliated projects, Michael has repeatedly transformed complexity into clarity and volatility into vision.

At the core of his leadership is an ability to bring financial insight and operational execution into perfect alignment. Whether guiding a company through a high-stakes recapitalization or designing scalable infrastructure for real-time decision-making, he leads from a place of strategic foresight and disciplined execution. He's known not just for his technical mastery, but for building cultures of accountability, trust, and shared ownership.

Previously, Michael was brought in to guide a rapidly growing company that faced mounting liquidity pressures, bond underwriting challenges, and internal misalignment. He led the financial restructuring efforts that unlocked millions in working capital, while also designing systems for predictive cashflow visibility across multiple business units. By aligning capital deployment with strategic priorities—not politics—he helped position the company for multi-million-dollar government contract fulfillment and long-term valuation growth.

In another transformative role, he led the full financial redesign of a technology firm seeking to leap from early traction to enterprise scale. Michael introduced AI-powered accounting infrastructure that enabled reporting within 24 to 48 hours of transaction activity—giving leadership real-time clarity into margin drivers, cash velocity, and unit economics. These systems didn't just improve reporting—they reshaped how the company thought about growth. His work contributed to a nine-figure increase in valuation and established the operational backbone for scaling across financial services.

Michael has also led product companies during times of extreme uncertainty, including global supply chain disruption. Facing broken logistics networks and unstable vendor relationships, he reimagined fulfillment and procurement by breaking down workflows into flexible, substitutable service modules. In under a year, he helped drive eight-figure revenue growth, navigating complex trade finance structures, international regulations, and rapid customer onboarding. His leadership extended beyond financial strategy—into hands-on operations, ethical compliance, and real-time problem solving across borders.

Earlier in his career, Michael operated at the highest levels of institutional finance, managing billions in liquidity and executing advanced forecasting strategies across asset classes, regulatory frameworks, and risk domains. He oversaw global cash positions, structured funding portfolios, and spearheaded treasury modernization efforts that redefined how institutions responded to evolving regulatory demands. From building high-yield repo books to implementing data-driven liquidity systems, Michael's tenure in global banking reflected both precision and adaptability.

Yet, through all of this, Michael's leadership philosophy remains grounded in people. He is a strong advocate of "earned clarity"—a leadership principle built on transparency, feedback, and relentless simplification. In his teams, simplicity is never mistaken for lack of sophistication—it's seen as a mark of maturity. He designs environments where team members understand not just *what* needs to be done, but *why* it matters—and where ownership is distributed, not hoarded.

He consistently emphasizes psychological safety as a cornerstone of performance. In his view, no financial model or operating framework can outperform a culture where people are afraid to speak up. He leads with openness, owns his mistakes publicly, and invites challenge in service of stronger outcomes. His belief that "you are not your output" echoes throughout the teams he builds—replacing performative busyness with meaningful, measurable impact.

Michael's contributions extend into the classroom, where he has taught corporate finance, capital markets, and mergers and acquisitions to future leaders and students. He holds a Global MBA in Entrepreneurship and a bachelor's degree in Banking, and is fluent in both English and German, with cross-cultural expertise shaped by years of international experience.

LinkedIn: https://www.linkedin.com/in/brinker-michael/

Chapter Nine

The Hero Leader's Path- Building a People-First Culture

Sarah Young

When I co-founded Premier Business Services, I made a promise to myself and my team: we would never become just another company that talks about people-first values but fails to live them. In today's business landscape, "culture" is more than a buzzword-it's the engine that drives sustainable growth, innovation, and fulfillment for everyone involved. But culture doesn't build itself. It requires intentional leadership, unwavering commitment to core values, and the courage to make tough decisions. This chapter is a candid look at how we put people first at Premier Business Services, how we nurture hero leaders at every level, and how those choices shape our journey.

People-First: More Than a Slogan

Our people-first philosophy starts with our mission, vision, and values. These aren't just posters on the wall-they're the standards by which we operate internally and the lens through which we allow clients to interact with our team. It's easy to say you're people-first; it's much harder to prove it when the rubber meets the road.

We emphasize how our team treats one another, but just as importantly, we set boundaries for how clients treat our people. If a client relationship threatens the well-being or growth of our team, we're willing to walk away. Protecting our culture sometimes means making hard calls, like parting ways with "bad eggs" who don't align with our values. Recently, we went through a real-time culture reset, removing a few misaligned individuals. The result? Stronger leadership, better collaboration, and a healthier team dynamic.

This experience reinforced a critical truth: no matter how robust your systems and values, the wrong people can derail your culture. You must be willing to act decisively to protect what matters most. Communication is the linchpin-enough transparency to build trust and buy-in, but not so much that it overwhelms or paralyzes decision-making. Especially as we scale, maintaining this rhythm is essential.

Ultimately, having the right people in the right roles makes everything else click. You can lead a horse to water, but you can't make it drink. If someone isn't on board with the mission, no amount of culture or communication will fix it. You'll always be putting out fires, sacrificing your company's momentum and the well-being of those who are aligned. Hero leaders recognize this and act accordingly.

Aligning Company Growth with Individual Growth

True alignment between business growth and individual employee growth doesn't happen by accident. It starts with clarity and a willingness to make hard decisions. I'm not afraid of employee turnover. In fact, I believe turnover gets a bad rap. In a company that's growing, evolving, and redefining its values, you have to be willing to hire and fire in service of progress.

We've made hires that looked perfect on paper-great energy, solid backgrounds, all the right words. But sometimes, those people weren't happy or brought toxic behaviors that cost us good team members. The red flags are there: frequent job-hopping without clear reasons, blaming others, or showing up with a "why this won't work" mindset instead of "how can I help?"

Alignment isn't just about training or professional development-it's about protecting your team. That means being crystal clear about expectations and holding everyone, leaders included, accountable. Our best employees want us to make those tough calls. They don't want to work alongside someone who checks out, gossips, or takes advantage.

When your team knows you're committed to the mission-and to the people who genuinely live it-that's when real alignment happens. Not just with your goals, but with each other. Hero leaders don't shy away from these conversations. They lean in, knowing that clarity and accountability are acts of service to the whole team.

Nurturing and Retaining High-Potential Talent

At Premier Business Services, we've revamped our approach to focus on the whole person-not just the employee. We have intentional conversations about each team member's personal, professional, and financial goals, so we can help them grow in ways that align with both their ambitions and our company's vision.

Our organizational chart isn't just a static diagram. It's a living map that helps team members see where they are, where they're going, and where they could go. We want people to know they have room to grow-and that we're paying attention to whether their current role is the right fit or if they're ready for something more advanced.

As a leader of multiple businesses, I have to remain agile and attuned to different team dynamics. One of the best decisions I made was bringing on a strong Operations Manager to work directly with our team. Their role is to ensure our people feel supported as professionals and as humans. When someone is thriving at home and at work, they bring their best self to the table.

I don't believe in "balance" as everything being equal. I believe in being present and intentional wherever you are. Whether it's work, family, or your own development, alignment and focus matter more than juggling.

We've also learned hard lessons around jealousy or resistance to others' success. Sometimes, people mock or diminish the very growth we've worked so hard to achieve. My advice: If you're no longer aligned with a company's direction, it's okay to seek out a team or mission that inspires you. Staying and criticizing only paints you in the wrong light. Realigning with something you can truly believe in is empowering.

Hero leaders lead by example. I won't get every detail perfect, but I'm moving toward the big picture I committed to-and that clears a path for others to move forward too.

Promoting Transparency and Trust-Especially in Challenging Times

Communication is not one-size-fits-all, especially in times of change or growth. Some team members want to focus on their day-to-day responsibilities; big-picture conversations can feel distracting or overwhelming. Others want every detail so they can map themselves into the vision and anticipate what's next. Finding the balance is a constant challenge.

We've built multiple communication layers to bridge these gaps. Our task management system outlines what we do for each client and who's responsible for what, across every role. This transparency helps everyone see how their work fits into the company and ensures that when responsibilities shift, expectations are still clear.

We also use a ticketing system for client requests and issues. This not only keeps us organized but creates learning opportunities across the team. Employees can review how past issues were handled, which builds confidence and supports cross-training.

Beyond systems, we stay connected through group chats, scheduled meetings, leadership discussions, and regular one-on-ones. These touchpoints ensure each team member is moving forward-not just within their role, but with the company as a whole.

I encourage employees to ask about the long-term vision. Those conversations push us to communicate more clearly, uncover blind spots, and build a stronger, more aligned team. Transparency isn't about oversharing-it's about creating enough clarity that people feel safe, valued, and confident in where we're headed, even during tough times. Hero leaders know that trust is built in the small moments, not just the big announcements.

Core Values as the Foundation of Hero Leadership

Our leadership is guided by a set of core values that we strive to live out every day. We're not perfect, but we're committed to getting better. These values shape how I lead, how we build our culture, and how we show up for each other and our clients:

- **Accountability:** We own our actions and follow through. When accountability is part of the culture, trust follows.

- **Quality:** We aim for high-quality work, taking pride in what we deliver. We're always learning, refining, and raising the bar-even if it means slowing down to get it right.
- **Culture:** Protecting our culture is an ongoing effort. One misaligned person can impact the whole team. We're committed to creating a space where people feel valued, respected, and energized to grow.
- **Results:** We're results-driven, but we define success thoughtfully. It's not about burnout or speed for the sake of speed-it's about setting clear goals, working with intention, and adjusting as we learn what works.
- **Communication:** Communication is always a work in progress. We're constantly finding ways to strike the right balance through open dialogue, systems, and transparency.
- **Discipline:** Discipline is about consistency, not perfection. We're building strong habits, staying focused, and sticking to what we say we'll do-even when things are messy or uncertain.

Flawless execution is always the goal, but it's unrealistic to expect perfection from anyone. What matters is our commitment to growth and continuous improvement. These values are our foundation. Every step we take to better live them strengthens our culture, our leadership, and our team.

The Hero Leader's Legacy

People-first, hero leader-driven leadership isn't about grand gestures or perfect execution. It's about showing up every day with intention, courage, and humility. It's about making the tough calls to protect your culture, investing in your people as whole humans, and building trust through transparency and accountability.

At Premier Business Services, we're still on this journey. We celebrate our wins, learn from our missteps, and remain committed to the big picture we set out to achieve. Hero leaders aren't born-they're made in the trenches, one decision at a time. By putting people first, we build not just a successful company, but a place where everyone can become the hero of their own story.

"If you want to go fast, go alone. If you want to go far, go together."

At Premier Business Services, we choose to go together-- one hero leader at a time.

Insta: https://www.instagram.com/sarah_premier/

Scan the QR code to listen to my interview on
"C-Suite Success with Tricia Benn."

About the Author

Sarah Young

With a degree in Accounting and Economics (specializing in Financial Economics) and a minor in Marketing, Sarah brings over 20 years of accounting experience across diverse sectors, including retail, banking, property management, agriculture, and utilities. In 2003, Sarah launched her bookkeeping career and later co-founded Premier Business Services, a bookkeeping, tax and business firm, with her business partner, Andrea. Alongside her husband, Sarah manages a portfolio of businesses, including Align Business Development, real estate ventures, & utility companies. As a dedicated mother of two, she enjoys teaching her children about business and spending quality family time.

Insta: https://www.instagram.com/sarah_premier/

Chapter Ten

Rising from the Ashes—Art, Faith, and Heroic Leadership

Dr. Scott Peck

In the hush of a museum gallery, as you stand before a painting that captures the agony of the crucifixion or the hope of resurrection, there is a sacred pause. It's a moment that transcends space and time. For me, that moment is the purpose—the still, small voice that drives everything I do. As an art historian and Executive Director of the Museum of Biblical Art, hero leadership begins not with ambition, but with reverence. Reverence for history, for culture, for humanity, and for the divine truths that connect us all.

Hero leadership, at its core, is not about power or prestige. It's about standing at the intersection of conviction and action— especially when the path is difficult, or even lonely. Leading a nonprofit institution in today's divided cultural landscape demands not just courage but a soul-deep resilience. For me, that resilience is rooted in Judeo-Christian values and the eternal truths of Scripture. These values don't merely influence my leadership; they define it.

Art as Moral Compass

I believe the Humanities—music, literature, dance, poetry, opera, ballet, and especially visual arts—offer society a way back to its moral compass. Our museum is not just a gallery of beautiful objects; it is a living, breathing institution designed to teach truth. Biblical art tells the stories that form the bedrock of Western ethics: the fidelity of Ruth, the courage of Esther, the mercy of the Good Samaritan, the justice of Moses.

Our mission is to present these narratives in a way that fosters education, dialogue, and transformation. I curate exhibitions not just to inform, but to awaken. When someone stands before a depiction of the parting of the Red Sea or the agony of Job, I want them to see themselves—to feel something move within that says, "This is the kind of person I want to be. This is the kind of world I want to live in." The Museum of Biblical Art is uniquely positioned to use the arts to teach vital values that I cherish. I can lead and help mold the generations to come by creating and displaying exhibitions that educate and foster principles like telling the truth, being faithful to your partner, not cheating, keeping your word, not stealing, and so on and so on.

This, I believe, is hero leadership: taking on the role of the cultural and moral educator at a time when the world desperately needs both.

Standing Firm in the Fire

Of course, not all leadership moments are in the spotlight. Some of the most formative ones are forged in the fire—sometimes quite literally.

Years ago, the museum I worked in suffered a catastrophic fire. A 30-year-old building without a sprinkler system, filled with priceless works of art, turned to ash. It was total destruction. Our leadership had been working on raising the funds for a fire suppression system, but we failed to do this is in time and we lost everything. There are no manuals for that kind of heartbreak, no rehearsals for that kind of public failure. But in the midst of the ruin, something extraordinary happened: the community rallied. People didn't run away—they ran toward us.

As the embers cooled, I knew this was a crucible moment—not just for the museum, but for me as a leader. We raised $9 million dollars and rebuilt. In four years, we did what would normally take a decade or more. Learning experiences included so many varied lessons where I had to develop expertise in fundraising, museum architecture, HVAC systems, landscape architecture, gallery design, collection acquisitions, fundraising, grant writing and insurance settlement negotiations. Some of the artwork did survive and that is how I developed my skills as an art conservator in repairing and restoring artwork.

I see it now as a story of resurrection. A phoenix story. It reminds me that failure isn't the opposite of success—it is the soil in which success takes root. That fire burned away everything but our purpose, and in its place, we rebuilt a sanctuary for art, education, and healing. In fact, we rose again—bigger, better, and with a deeper sense of mission.

The rebuilding wasn't simply about bricks and mortar. It was spiritual. It was emotional. Every decision we made—from architectural layout to curatorial direction—was grounded in prayer, discernment, and collaboration. We asked not just, "What should we build?" but "Who do we want to become?" Hero leaders ask that question daily.

When It's Hard to Stand, Stand Anyway

True hero leadership means standing for your values even when it costs you. Especially when it costs you.

Our organization's values involve teaching understanding and acceptance of people of all faiths and backgrounds. Antisemitism is a challenge today. Our country was built on the idea of freedom of religion, and this includes Judaism or the Jewish faith. In recent years, our museum took a public and profound stand against antisemitism. This was not a trendy stance; it was a necessary one. As an institution rooted in biblical traditions, it was imperative for us to affirm the dignity and legacy of the Jewish people. We launched a series of Holocaust-themed art exhibitions—not simply to memorialize the past, but to speak truth to the present.

That's how the Museum of Holocaust Art was born—the first museum of its kind to teach the Holocaust through artwork rather than traditional means. In our galleries, visitors don't just read facts; they feel the emotional weight of history. Our other exhibitions use artwork to teach against misogyny, racial inequality, and other forms of hate speech and hate crime. The ideas of standing up for women, battling discrimination against African Americans, Asians or Hispanics, helping the poor, rescuing animals, reforming criminals, aiding widows and orphans, and other social actions can be difficult and very unpopular these days in the United States. Many people today almost feel as if they have permission to spew hate speech or perform a hate crime. Through artwork I strive to lead by example through hero leadership, attempting to change, reform, and transform our very core values, teaching appreciation and respect for all people and all belief systems.

This, too, is hero leadership: creating platforms for others to find their voice, their healing, and their courage.

The feedback we've received has been overwhelming—and humbling. Survivors, family members, students, and international guests have walked into our spaces and wept. They've written notes, sent letters, and shared stories that now become part of our legacy. That's the impact of art, and that's the charge of every hero leader: to hold space for truth, no matter how painful.

Building a Culture of Bravery

Every nonprofit leader knows that resources are scarce, needs are great, and expectations are sky-high. My advice to emerging leaders is this: lead with heart, but also with hands. Be brave enough to feel, but bold enough to act.

Too many leaders wait for perfect conditions to collaborate. I believe in jumping in—with both feet and an open heart. Let's be friends. Let's share our stories of failure and success. Let's dream out loud. Collaboration isn't a buzzword; it's a survival strategy. When we give first—our time, our wisdom, our connections—we often receive more than we ever imagined. My heart always wants to give back to those that give to me and my nonprofit. I hope I radiate a mission driven charisma that overtakes you, making you even more zealous about your own mission and identity.

One of the secrets to our museum's success has been relentless collaboration. We've worked with over 50 museums nationwide—science museums, train museums, art museums, historic homes—because I believe we are stronger together. It's not just about what we can achieve; it's about what we can awaken in one another.

True bravery in leadership is about stewarding relationships, not just results. It's choosing character over convenience. It's saying yes to uncomfortable conversations and "no" to shortcuts that compromise the mission. Hero leaders live in integrity—and that integrity builds trust that echoes far beyond any single project or exhibition.

Living the Mission Every Day

As Executive Director, I wear many hats: curator, educator, fundraiser, ambassador. But more than anything, I am the guardian of the mission. I am the storyteller. And not just of biblical tales—but of our institutional identity.

When I speak with donors, I'm not pitching a project. I'm sharing a vision. When I engage with visitors, I'm not giving a tour. I'm igniting imagination. When I train staff or volunteers, I'm not managing tasks. I'm shaping a movement.

Our museum is not just a building. It's a place where souls are stirred. And that only happens when leadership is rooted in passion, integrity, and an unshakable sense of purpose.

In every staff meeting and boardroom, I try to embody what I expect of others: humility, accountability, and a genuine hunger to serve. The moment a leader stops learning, they stop leading. Hero leaders are forever students—of history, of people, of the divine.

Hero leadership creates strong relationships. My drive and feverish emotions solidify and unify our staff to act and change the world through art exhibitions and art education, teaching desperately needed values to a confused world that seems to have lost it moral compass.

Leadership is Legacy

Perhaps the most profound lesson I've learned is that hero leadership is not about what you build—it's about what you leave behind.

Every exhibit we open, every student we educate, every artifact we preserve is part of a larger legacy. I often think about the young person who walks into our gallery for the first time. Maybe they've never seen art like this. Maybe they've never heard these stories. Maybe, in that moment, something inside them comes alive.

That is why I lead. That is why I get up every morning and do the work—even when it's hard, even when I'm tired. Because in this world full of noise, art has the power to whisper truth. And through that whisper, lives can change.

A Final Word to Fellow Leaders

If you're reading this and wondering if you have what it takes to be a hero leader—let me assure you: you do. Heroism is not about perfection. It's about presence. It's about being faithful to the mission, especially when the fire comes.

Lead with your values. Fight for what matters. Collaborate with courage. And above all, never forget why you started.

Let your passion permeate every part of your organization. Let your story be the thread that connects people to a purpose greater than themselves. And when you rise from your own ashes—and you will—don't just rebuild. Rebuild with vision. Rebuild with love. Rebuild like a hero.

Because in the end, the world doesn't need more executives. It needs more leaders who are willing to stand in the fire, hold the light, and tell the truth through every canvas, every word, and every act of courage.

Scan the QR code to listen to my interview on "C-Suite Success with Tricia Benn."

About the Author

Dr. Scott Peck

Dr. Scott Peck is an Art Historian, Art Educator and Art Conservator. With over 25 years of experience, he has curated over 200 Museum Exhibitions. Highlights include Marc Chagall, French Impressionists, Norman Rockwell, Michelangelo, the Dead Sea Scrolls, Salvador Dali, and Andy Warhol. He has worked with over 50 different Museums throughout the United States such as plane museums, train museums, science museums, history museums, art museums, and historic home museums. Dr. Peck has written over 30 Publications including books, art catalogues and academic journal articles. Experience in media production include many films, movies, and Emmy award winning television programs. On the university level he has been Adjunct Faculty and Doctoral Fellow at the University of North Texas. Dr. Peck is currently the Executive Director of the Museum of Biblical Art, Museum of Holocaust Art, and the National Center for Jewish Art in Dallas, TX.

Chapter Eleven

The Hero Leader's Mindset

Sheila Rondeau

Leadership isn't about titles. It's not about power. It's about stepping up, taking risks, and making things happen—even when the odds are against you. It's about looking at uncertainty and saying, "Let's go." That's what it means to lead like a hero.

As a combat veteran and a business leader, I've learned that the principles of leadership are universal. The battlefield and the boardroom may look different, but they both demand decisiveness, resilience, and the ability to inspire people to move in the right direction—especially when things get tough. You don't wait for the perfect plan or the ideal conditions. You act. You adjust. You lead.

Knowing Your Team, Knowing Yourself

One of the fundamental lessons from military leadership is simple: Know your people. Understand their strengths, weaknesses, and motivations. This applies to your employees, your partners, and even your clients. You need to anticipate their needs before they do and adjust accordingly.

In business, you'll work with people who are analytical, people who are impulsive, people who thrive on structure, and people who resist it. Some companies foster a deep, cohesive culture, while others are a patchwork of different styles and personalities. Your job as a leader is to recognize what makes people tick and meet them where they are.

But knowing your team isn't enough. You have to know yourself, too. Where are you strongest? Where do you need to step back and let someone else take the lead? Leadership isn't about being the smartest person in the room—it's about creating an environment where the smartest ideas win. That takes confidence. It takes humility. And it takes courage.

Sometimes, that also means mentoring your team in real time. At MOGXP, I make it a point to include one or two team members on high-level projects so they can learn directly from me. This fosters a culture of hands-on growth, builds their confidence, and empowers them to take on greater responsibilities as we scale.

Decision-Making in the Face of Chaos

If there's one thing I've learned, it's this: Time is your biggest enemy. When things go sideways, the worst thing you can do is freeze. Instead, you move quickly, decisively, and with purpose.

I've been in situations where natural disasters threatened entire marketing activations—wildfires, tornadoes, hurricanes, you name it. I've had clients who needed an entirely new strategy overnight. And every single time, the key to success was the same: Cut through the noise, identify the decision-makers, and execute. No hesitation. No overanalyzing. No second-guessing. Failure is not an option.

It's not about being reckless; it's about being efficient. Layers of management and endless deliberation will kill momentum. You don't have time for that. If you're leading a company, you have to make the call and stand by it. Adjust, when necessary, but don't waver. The team takes its cues from you. If you're confident, they'll move with you.

One of the most challenging decisions I've had to make was finding the balance between working *in* the business and working *on* the business. As the CEO, I'm both the visionary and the expert. But that doesn't mean I should do everything myself. A hero leader trains others to carry the torch, invests in their growth, and learns to delegate so the company can evolve.

Creating Disruption Through Strategic Risk

Disruption isn't about being different for the sake of being different. It's about solving problems in a way no one else has thought of. In my industry, experiential marketing, a lot of people focus on creativity and storytelling. That's important. But I approach it differently—I see it through the lens of logistics, math, and execution. How can we maximize impact with the resources we have? How can we streamline, optimize, and still blow people away?

That's where the hero leader mindset comes in. You take risks, but they're calculated. You push boundaries, but with purpose. And most importantly, you stay true to your brand and your values. Authenticity isn't just a buzzword—it's the foundation of credibility. If you aren't walking the talk, people will see right through you.

I started MOGXP because I saw the inefficiencies in traditional agencies and knew there was a better way. I didn't just want to do things differently—I wanted to do them better. That mindset of disruption is what fueled my entrepreneurial journey and what continues to guide how I lead today.

Balancing the Levers of Life and Business

People love to talk about work-life balance like it's some kind of static equation. It's not. It's a set of levers that you constantly adjust based on what's happening in your life and business. There are times when your career demands everything from you. There are times when personal responsibilities take priority. The key is knowing which levers to push and pull at the right time.

That means making tough decisions. Saying yes to one thing means saying no to another. But here's the real trick—once you make a choice, own it. No regrets. No second-guessing. You commit, and you move forward.

You also have to be honest about what brings value. I often ask myself, "What's the impact?" If a program, project, or even a partnership isn't contributing to our greater goal, then it's time to reconsider. Sometimes, the most powerful move is stepping away.

Building a Culture of Hero Leadership

A true hero leader doesn't just focus on their own success. They build a culture where leadership is embedded at every level. This means fostering an environment where people feel empowered to take initiative, make decisions, and push boundaries. You can't micromanage greatness—you have to trust your team to rise to the occasion.

Encouraging leadership at all levels means creating space for innovation. It means allowing team members to experiment, to try new ideas, and even to fail—because failure is often the stepping stone to breakthroughs. Great leaders recognize that the best ideas don't always come from the top. They come from the people who are in the trenches, dealing with challenges firsthand.

When you cultivate an environment where people feel safe to take calculated risks, you foster a culture of resilience and adaptability. You create an organization that is constantly evolving, growing, and pushing the envelope of what's possible.

We build this culture every day at MOGXP. One thing that's helped us is a simple, consistent touchpoint: daily working sessions. Everyone can pop in, share updates, talk through challenges, and brainstorm. It keeps us agile, transparent, and in sync.

The Satisfaction of the Win

There's a moment that every hero leader knows well—the moment after the storm, when everything has fallen into place, and you can finally step back and take it in. I've stood in warehouses at 3 AM, watching trucks roll out for a national campaign that people said couldn't be done. And because I wasn't ready to leave yet, I grabbed a broom and swept the floor. I just needed to soak in what we had accomplished. It was fun and I wasn't ready to share that with everyone yet, and afterwards we did. We had our high fives, and we had our celebrations. But sometimes you need to soak in what you accomplished.

Leadership isn't about the spotlight. It's about the mission. It's about the impact. And at the end of the day, it's about knowing that you stood up, took the risk, and led your team to something greater than they thought was possible. That's what it means to be a hero leader.

The Never-Ending Evolution of a Hero Leader

Being a hero leader isn't a one-time achievement. It's a continuous journey of growth, learning, and evolution. Markets change, industries shift, and new challenges arise every day. The leaders who thrive are the ones who are always learning, always adapting, and always ready to face the next challenge head-on.

Think of it like a puzzle. What are the pieces that you need to have to be successful? How do they fit? Do you have the right people in the right spots? Do you have the right suppliers at the right budget? When you get done going through the puzzle pieces, you should be able to go through every one of those items and understand which ones need to change. Sometimes it means people change roles. Sometimes it means changing the timeline, changing the budget or seeing that the path you're on, is not the one that leads to your goals. Take a different path, but be strong enough to do it, and if you do make that change, commit to it and move forward and don't whine about it.

If you want to lead like a hero, don't get too comfortable. Comfort breeds complacency, and complacency kills momentum. Stay curious, stay hungry, and never stop pushing yourself to be better. Read books, listen to new perspectives, and surround yourself with people who challenge you.

At MOGXP, one way I foster this mindset is by recommending books that shaped my own journey—like *The Power of Who* by Bob Beaudine. It helps us grow as individuals and as a team. Learning together builds unity, trust, and alignment around a shared purpose.

Above all, remember this: Leadership is not about being invincible. It's about being unstoppable. It's about showing up, stepping up, and making things happen—even when the odds are against you. That's what defines a true hero leader.

Scan the QR code to listen to my interview on
"C-Suite Success with Tricia Benn."

About the Author

Sheila Rondeau

As the visionary behind MOGXP, Sheila Rondeau offers dual expertise as a Fractional CMO and experiential marketing strategist. Her data-driven approach ensures measurable ROI while maintaining creative excellence across both service areas.

After decades working with major brands, Sheila launched MOGXP (Marketing Operations Group Experiential), a boutique marketing agency. She divides her focus between hands-on CMO consulting services for growing businesses and delivering innovative experiential campaigns for established brands.

Sheila's expertise in operations, logistics, and leadership enables her to provide strategic CMO guidance while implementing mobile marketing, product sampling, pop-up retail, and VIP experiences that exceed business objectives. As a Fractional CMO, she helps companies build sustainable marketing infrastructures while her experiential work drives consumer engagement.

Before MOGXP, Sheila managed Anheuser-Busch's mobile marketing program and designed impactful cause campaigns like "Tide Loads of Hope." Her military background- 20 years of U.S. Army service including combat in the First Gulf War-- shaped her leadership approach. She specialized in logistics and operations--skills she now applies to both Fractional CMO work and experiential marketing execution.

Based in Dallas, Sheila splits her time between strategic CMO consulting and overseeing experiential campaigns. She mentors the next generation of marketing professionals while maintaining personalized service and the strategic insight that defines MOGXP's balanced approach to marketing excellence.

Notable Client Partnerships
SONY, Kellogg's, Chevrolet
DIAGEO, UPS, Toyota
CVS, Rite Aid, Ben & Jerry's
Proctor & Gamble, ESSENCE Magazine
Coca-Cola, Optimum-Nutrition, BSN
Unilever, Johnson & Johnson, ThunderShirts
Isopure, GlaxoSmithKline, Diamond Foods

sheila@mogxp.com
LinkedIn: https://www.linkedin.com/in/sheilarondeau/

Chapter Twelve

Leading with Heart

Thomas A. Schmidt

Success in business is often measured in financial terms—revenue, profits, market share. But true success, the kind that sustains over decades and changes lives, is measured in impact. It is measured in the number of people you serve and how well you serve them. A hero leader understands this distinction and leads not just with strategy, but with heart.

The Hero Leader's Blueprint

A hero leader is someone who pledges to lead with integrity, transparency, and a commitment to giving back to their communities. They understand that leadership is not about authority but about responsibility. In my journey through leadership, spanning over three decades in the financial industry, I have come to define success not by the size of my company but by the relationships I have built and the lives I have impacted.

For me, success has always been about service. I ask myself a simple question at the end of each day: *Are you better off for having met me today?* This mindset has been the foundation of my leadership and has shaped every decision I make. Whether it is a client in need, an employee seeking guidance, or a partner looking for direction, my goal is always to provide value beyond what is expected.

Leading with Integrity and Purpose

One of the earliest leadership lessons I learned was that people don't care how much you know until they know how much you care. This principle has been at the core of my leadership philosophy. It is not about titles or accolades; it is about character and integrity. If you lead with these principles, success—both in business and in life—will follow.

Integrity means doing the right thing, even when no one is watching. It means making decisions that are in the best interest of your employees, your clients, and your community, rather than simply chasing profits. It also means being transparent—communicating openly and honestly, even when the news isn't good.

A hero leader understands that their job is not just to lead, but to lift others up. Be willing to give and expect nothing in return. I believe in leading by example, whether that means taking on a small task to help a team member or listening to an employee's concerns with genuine empathy. Leadership is not about delegating from the top down; it is about walking alongside your team and showing them what is possible.

The Power of Emotional Intelligence

One of the most overlooked aspects of leadership is emotional intelligence—the ability to connect with people on a deeper level. Understanding your employees, recognizing their strengths and weaknesses, and helping them grow is crucial. People will go to the ends of the earth for a leader they trust, respect, and feel appreciated by.

Depending on the size of the company, the CEO's leadership role will be different. In a smaller company, employees have a more personal connection directly with the CEO. For a larger organization that has a management team with different departments, the CEO can foster an environment where emotional intelligence is valued and practiced with mentorship, training programs or simply leading by example.

The better the CEO and his/her leadership team listen to their teams, the better the results for the company in not only employee morale, but also in overall productivity. When you have the right personnel working in the right positions inside a company, you will always have great results.

A great leader also understands that different employees require different leadership styles. Some employees need hands-on guidance, while others thrive with autonomy. Early in my career I learned that leadership lesson from my manager. He recognized that while I had great skills for his company, my skills could serve a greater good if I was somewhere else. That realization changed my life forever, but more importantly it has had a profound impact on the hundreds of people my company has had the privilege of serving.

Recognizing these differences and adapting accordingly allows a leader to build a more effective and motivated team. This ability to read people and adjust your approach when dealing with employees or clients, is what sets great leaders apart from good ones.

Navigating Change with Resilience

Change is inevitable, it is what you do with it that matters, especially in today's business world. The key to navigating uncertainty is adaptability. As a leader, you must recognize what you can control and what you cannot. When faced with challenges—whether it be economic downturns, technological disruptions, or internal struggles—the focus should always be on the fundamentals. Identify what truly matters, make strategic adjustments, and surround yourself with people you trust to have the knowledge and expertise you may lack.

I believe the leadership style changes depending on the situation. If a company experiences a drop in sales, for example, often it becomes necessary to get back to the basics – identifying what you can control and what you cannot. Perhaps adjustments in the marketplace need to be made and determining whether or not it still fits your target market. The crucial point is to focus on the processes you can control.

For changes such as the ever-evolving world of technology, digital marketing and artificial intelligence, it is important for a leader to recognize what they don't know and either hire for that need or find a way to outsource that to someone who specializes in that area. Change is inevitable and leaders need to find ways to adapt accordingly.

At times, leadership means making difficult decisions, but it also means knowing when to listen and learn. The best leaders are perpetual students. They seek knowledge from peers, from mentors, and from their own experiences. They understand that growth never stops and that the moment you believe you know it all is the moment you begin to fail.

As a leader, I try my best to stay humble in all things and always do the right thing the first time and to put other people's needs ahead of my own. The times I have forgotten those principles are the times when the situations did not work out well. When I provide more benefit, than what was expected or anticipated, without expecting anything in return, to the client, their employees and those we serve, then we succeed as a company.

Change can bring uncertainty. Employees look to their leaders for reassurance during times of uncertainty. A steady, confident, resilient leader can help a team navigate even the most turbulent of times. By remaining level-headed and solution-focused, a leader can instill confidence in their team and keep morale high.

Leaving a Legacy

Hero leadership is not about the wealth you accumulate; it is about the impact you leave behind. My father ran a successful flower shop and as I grew up, he taught me the ins and outs of running a business. When my father passed away at 52 years old, our family faced struggles that could have been avoided if there had been a business succession plan in place. Unfortunately, my father always thought there would be another day in which he could develop one. But life doesn't happen that way. That experience shaped my career and my mission—to help others avoid the same pitfalls. If I can help take my client's burden off their plate, even just for a little while, then I am living in my principles. My purpose is in serving others, and in doing so, success follows naturally.

Every leader must find their *why*—the reason they wake up each morning and push forward. For me, it has always been about service. Whether guiding a business owner through succession planning or helping an employee find their true potential, I see my role as lifting the burden off others so they can focus on what matters most.

The true mark of success as a leader is not how many people work for you, but how many people are better off because of you. Lead with integrity, serve with humility, and never stop learning. That is the essence of hero leadership.

The Continuous Journey of a Hero Leader

Being a hero leader is not a destination; it is a journey. It requires constant reflection and improvement. It means taking the time to assess your own growth as a leader and recognizing areas where you can do better. It means mentoring the next generation of leaders and instilling in them the same values that have guided you.

It is also about finding balance. As leaders, we often put others before ourselves, but true hero leadership also requires self-care. Taking time to recharge, to reflect, and to continue learning ensures that we can keep leading effectively. Burnout is real, and even the most dedicated leader cannot pour from an empty cup.

Hero leaders create organizations that outlive them. They build cultures of integrity, service, and continuous growth. They leave behind legacies that inspire others to lead with purpose. And above all, they make the world a little better each day by asking themselves one simple question: *Are you better off for having met me today?*

Scan the QR code to listen to my interview on
"C-Suite Success with Tricia Benn."

About the Author

Thomas A. Schmidt

Thomas A. Schmidt, CFBS, CLTC, LACP, CEPA (https://aha.pub/TomSchmidt) has been in the financial services industry for over 35 years. After receiving his Bachelor's in Business Administration from Kansas State University in 1982, he worked as an analyst for Amoco Production Company before entering the financial service industry in 1988. Since then, he has worked for many industry giants, including MassMutual, American United Life, and Paul Revere Insurance.

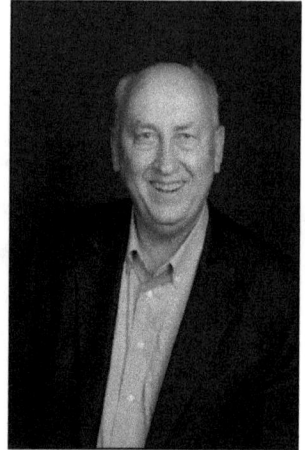

He has held many industry leadership positions, received numerous awards, certifications, and licenses as a financial professional and insurance specialist.

Tom has an incredible knowledge of the market and a thorough understanding of contract details. Still, the greatest passion in his career is helping people take care of themselves and their families. He takes on the role of teacher and counselor to his clients, and he enjoys listening to their stories and getting to know them on a personal level.

Today his firm specializes in Employee Benefits, Long Term Care, Business Succession, Retirement and Estate Planning for

Businesses and individuals. Since starting his career, he has been a member of the National Association of Insurance and Financial Advisors (NAIFA), served as the Oklahoma City Chapter President and received the 2005 Oklahoma City Financial Advisor of the Year. He is also a Life and Qualifying Member of the prestigious Million Dollar Round Table (MDRT) organization and an Excalibur Knight in the MDRT Foundation. As a member of the National Association of Benefits and Insurance Professionals (NABIP) he has achieved the Leading Producer's Roundtable Soaring Eagle Award and is a life and qualifying member for being an elite producer at the National Level.

He is a lifetime member of the Kansas State University Alumni Association, Lambda Chi Alpha Social Fraternity, a brotherhood bond he shares with his son Michael, the Oklahoma City Chamber of Commerce and attends Crossings Community Church.

Tom has been involved with Boy Scouting since the age of eight and has served in many capacities as an adult including Cubmaster, Scoutmaster, Eagle Review Boards, Merit Badge Counselor, and the Baden Powell District Committee in the Last Frontier Council Boy Scouts of America. He and his son, Michael, also an Eagle Scout, are Lifetime Members of the National Eagle Scout Association. He has been awarded the Celtic Cross, Cubmaster of the Year, and the Scoutmaster Award of Merit for his service to youth and the James E West Fellowship Award.

To remember his father and the talents learned in the flower shop, Tom enjoys making Christmas wreaths for family, friends, and clients. He enjoys spending time with his wife, Terri, and their son Michael and daughter in law Haley traveling and going to college athletic events.

LinkedIn:

https://www.linkedin.com/in/tom-schmidt-831866b4/

Chapter Thirteen

The Leadership Edge: What It Takes to Succeed

Tricia Benn

Leadership is far more than just holding a title. It's about having the courage, resilience, and vision to drive meaningful impact. Over the course of my career, I've seen that exceptional leaders don't just manage a team; they inspire, innovate, and create environments where everyone can thrive. So, what sets apart the most successful leaders? It all starts with building a strong foundation.

A Mission That Matters

At the heart of great leadership is a mission that truly matters, not just to the executives, but their teams and the communities they serve. A strong mission fuels passion, attracts the right talent, and creates alignment across teams. When people believe in the work they're doing, they show up differently. They bring energy, commitment, and a deep sense of purpose to the table. The most successful leaders are the ones who can articulate their mission clearly and ensure that every team member understands their contributions and how they are valued.

When you genuinely care about the mission, moving things forward becomes a natural outcome. The best organizations aren't just driven by profits; they are propelled by purpose (and their people), which drives greater profitability. The financials are critical, but a strong mission creates a strong foundation for sustainable financial success.

That mission must be revisited frequently, not to change its core, but to renew its relevance and reinvigorate the team. In fast-paced industries, the ability to ground innovation in a stable, meaningful purpose is what allows teams to adapt without losing their way. Leadership is not about rigidly sticking to one course, but about ensuring that the compass -- the mission -- is always clear and guiding every decision.

Balancing Innovation and Stability

One of the biggest challenges any leader faces is finding the right balance between innovation and stability. Change is essential, but moving too fast without structure can lead to chaos. On the other hand, being overly cautious can stifle growth.

The key? Understand yourself first. Know your strengths, your risk tolerance, and where you thrive. Then, surround yourself with the right team, those who push for bold moves and those who ensure the details are covered. I structure my leadership team with a two-thirds-to-one-third ratio: two-thirds driving innovation and forward movement, and one-third focused on ensuring that change isn't happening for change's sake and focused on minimizing the associated risk.

This approach enables both momentum and precision. Innovation is the lifeblood of growth, but it must be executed with care. By honoring both visionaries and pragmatists, great leaders cultivate environments where change is meaningful and sustainable.

Lessons That Shape Leadership

One of the most valuable lessons I've learned as a leader is that people and financials are not separate priorities. They go hand in hand. When you put people first and ensure they are engaged, empowered, and aligned with the mission, financial success follows. The best leaders don't just talk about valuing their teams; they show it in their actions. They invest in professional development, recognize contributions, and foster a culture where people feel seen, heard, and celebrated.

Equally important? Staying close to our financials. A mission without financial health is either a fleeting dream or a path to martyrdom. Understanding cash flow, profitability, and sustainability allows leaders to make informed decisions and build long-term success.

Financial insight doesn't just benefit executives; it empowers the entire team. When people understand how their work contributes to the organization's success, they become invested in its sustainability and growth. This lesson is more than prioritizing people or financials independently; it is about realizing that they must work together. Keeping institutional knowledge within the team strengthens client relationships and drives greater profitability. This principle extends beyond employees. It also applies to clients and partners, reinforcing that success with people and financials is interconnected, not mutually exclusive.

Financial acumen should be used as a tool of empowerment, not punishment. When teams are trusted with information and understand how decisions impact outcomes, they rise to the occasion. Clarity in the numbers creates clarity in the mission. It turns metrics into motivators and transforms strategy into shared ownership.

Balancing Interests

A great CEO must balance the needs of everyone: shareholders, employees, customers, and the broader community. The secret? Creating alignment through values and trusted relationships.

At the C-SUITE NETWORK™, we believe in the power of trusted relationships. The currency of the future is not just financial capital, but the strength of the relationships we build. When we surround ourselves with people we trust -- those who share our mission and values -- we create a force multiplier for success.

That's why alignment is essential. When there's a clear, shared vision of what success looks like and how everyone contributes to it, competing interests start to dissolve. It's not about choosing one group over another; it's about ensuring that decisions create value across the board.

Our core values of **Relevancy, Reach, Reciprocity, and Respect** guide us in ensuring that every stakeholder -- from employees to customers to shareholders -- is part of a thriving, mission-driven ecosystem. When these values are embedded in the culture, they build trust, drive performance, and ensure long-term success for all involved.

Being a part of a trusted community like C-SUITE NETWORK™ reinforces that success isn't a solo act. It's about collaboration and contribution. When you walk your leadership journey alongside people who share your values, your mission becomes stronger, and the impact becomes exponential.

What Sets Exceptional CEOs Apart?

What truly distinguishes the best leaders from the rest? A few key qualities:

1. **Unwavering Values** – Exceptional leaders take a stand. They don't waver based on external pressures; they lead with integrity and make decisions that align with their principles.

2. **Empathy and Transparency** – They understand people, relate to their experiences, and communicate their commitments openly. Employees, customers, and stakeholders trust them because they are authentic and transparent about where they stand.

3. **Mission-Driven Leadership** – They continuously connect their teams to the bigger purpose, ensuring that every initiative, decision, and strategy aligns with the overarching mission.

4. **Financial Acumen** – Financial sustainability is the engine that drives growth and scale. The most exceptional CEOs master that balance—ensuring financial success while staying true to their values. Financial acumen shouldn't be a tool for control or restriction but an enabler of opportunity, empowering teams to innovate, take smart risks, and build lasting impact.

5. **Humility** – Great leaders recognize that they don't have all the answers. They stay curious, seek input, and surround themselves with people they trust. They listen not just to respond, but to understand. They grow alongside their teams, adapting, evolving, and constantly striving to be better. Leadership isn't about having all the solutions; it's about creating an environment where the best ideas rise, the right people step up, and everyone is empowered to contribute to something bigger than themselves.

6. **Celebrating Success** – They don't just drive results; they ensure that every win is shared. Seeing their people succeed is what fuels them, and they create a culture where everyone is recognized and valued.

At the end of the day, leadership is about impact. It's about creating something bigger than yourself, aligning people around a powerful mission, and ensuring that every decision contributes to sustainable success. The best leaders know that their role isn't just to direct but to inspire, empower, and create an environment where people can thrive in alignment with the organization's overall success and cement a deeper impact throughout the communities they serve.

Leadership is a lifelong commitment to growth, integrity, and influence. It's about showing up, not just when it's convenient, but especially when it's hard. And it's about leaving a legacy, not just in profits, but in people, values, and the impact we create.

Scan the QR code to listen to my podcast
"C-Suite Success with Tricia Benn."

About the Author

Tricia Benn

Chief Executive Officer, C-Suite Network | General Manager, The Hero Club | Transformational Business Leader & Growth Strategist

Tricia Benn is the Chief Executive Officer of the C-SUITE NETWORK™— the most influential network of business leaders—and General Manager of The Hero Club, an invitation-only organization for CEOs, founders, and investors committed to values-based leadership.

With a mission to accelerate the success of C-level executives, business owners, and investors, Tricia is leading the charge of building the C-SUITE NETWORK™ platform rooted in community, content, counsel, and commerce. She is dedicated to creating a trusted ecosystem where a values-based approach, bold collaboration, radical transparency, and unwavering integrity fuel measurable growth and lasting impact.

A top leadership development CEO and award-winning business strategist, Tricia is a dynamic force in transforming organizations through purpose-led leadership. Over the course of 25+ years, she has worked exclusively with high-level decision-makers across public, private, political, nonprofit, government, and faith-based sectors—driving strategies that deliver meaningful, measurable outcomes at the highest levels.

With a distinguished career spanning market research, telecommunications, media marketing, and advertising, Tricia has built and scaled high-performing divisions within billion-dollar enterprises and entrepreneurial ventures alike. Her proven track record of delivering double-digit, year-over-year growth is rooted in a unique ability to drive innovation, forge strategic partnerships, and lead transformative change.

Tricia's leadership has fueled success across diverse sectors—including manufacturing, healthcare, medical and dental practices, plastics, financial services, and pharmaceuticals—where she has helped both enterprise-level organizations and high-growth entrepreneurs unlock new levels of revenue, market influence, and operational excellence.

Prior to joining the C-SUITE NETWORK™, Tricia served as Global Chief Marketing & Strategy Officer and U.S. Managing Director for a $3 billion global holding company, where she led market expansions and secured landmark contracts with some of the world's most influential organizations.

As host of the podcast and TV show *C-Suite Success with Tricia Benn*, she delivers powerful, practical insights through exclusive conversations with elite business leaders—revealing the strategies behind real, lasting success.

Beyond her executive roles, Tricia serves on multiple business, industry, and nonprofit boards and is a trusted advisor and mentor to top executives navigating complex decisions, scaling their ventures, and building legacy-driven organizations.

Learn more at www.c-suitenetwork.com and The Hero Club. Connect with Tricia on LinkedIn, X, Instagram, or Facebook.

www.ingramcontent.com/pod-product-compliance
Lightning Source LLC
Chambersburg PA
CBHW030331220326
41518CB00048B/2232